ROUTLEDGE LIBRARY EDITIONS:
EARLY WESTERN RESPONSES
TO SOVIET RUSSIA

Volume 11

I0878398

RUSSIAN MINDS IN FETTERS

RUSSIAN MINDS IN FETTERS

S. MACKIEWICZ

Routledge
Taylor & Francis Group
LONDON AND NEW YORK

First published in 1932 by George Allen & Unwin Ltd

This edition first published in 2018
by Routledge
2 Park Square, Milton Park, Abingdon, Oxon OX14 4RN

and by Routledge
711 Third Avenue, New York, NY 10017

Routledge is an imprint of the Taylor & Francis Group, an informa business

British Library Cataloguing in Publication Data
A catalogue record for this book is available from the British Library

ISBN: 978-1-138-04993-2 (Set)
ISBN: 978-1-315-11072-1 (Set) (ebk)
ISBN: 978-1-138-07119-3 (Volume 11) (hbk)
ISBN: 978-1-138-07135-3 (Volume 11) (pbk)
ISBN: 978-1-315-11469-9 (Volume 11) (ebk)

Publisher's Note
The publisher has gone to great lengths to ensure the quality of this reprint but points out that some imperfections in the original copies may be apparent.

Disclaimer
The publisher has made every effort to trace copyright holders and would welcome correspondence from those they have been unable to trace.

RUSSIAN MINDS IN FETTERS

by

S. MACKIEWICZ

With an Introduction by

PRINCE EUSTACE SAPIEHA

LONDON

GEORGE ALLEN & UNWIN LTD

MUSEUM STREET

FIRST PUBLISHED IN 1932

PRINTED IN GREAT BRITAIN BY
UNWIN BROTHERS LTD., WOKING

CONTENTS

INTRODUCTION

It often happens that a mysterious disease cannot be defined even by clever doctors, and only a specialist in neurology can give a satisfactory diagnosis. In my opinion Mr. Mackiewicz has filled the part of just such a specialist, examining the case of Bolshevism. This verdict is "hysteria," and that alone would be nothing new, as many before him have described the complaint of Russia in very much the same words; but the analysis he gives us of that special form of hysteria is a masterpiece.

Soviet Russia has been described and discussed from the economic and sociological points of view; this is a study of the psychological side of the problem. It answers a hundred unanswered questions; it makes the whole problem clear.

Studying Bolshevism, we must not forget that our mind also is in fetters. Ours are the golden bonds of Christian morality, grafted on the heirloom of ancient Greece and Rome, bearing traces of a hundred civilizations which have crystallized into our present ethical standards. These standards are apt to blur our judgment on Bolshevism, because, dealing with Russia, we must use another code or run the risk of being partial. Bolsheviks are neither good nor bad, neither cruel nor kind, neither just nor unjust. Love, kindness, morality, pity and justice are equally banished from Bolshevia as well as the Christian inverse of those virtues. All those terms and conceptions are considered "bourgeois prejudice," and the Russian communists exert themselves successfully to train a people of a hundred and fifty millions into using a new code devoid of all Christian morality.

It is not only unfair to exaggerate the "atrocities" of the Soviets, it is also very unwise, and deceptive immorality at the worst is only a momentary rebellion against a ruling morality; the total absence of morality even without excesses, as is the case at this moment in Russia, is the dethroning of moral law, which is a great deal worse. That is why the objectivity of Mr. Mackiewicz is of so great a value. It shows clearly that we have to deal not with a violent, passing crisis, but with a chronic, spreading and lasting organic transformation.

Russian Minds in Fetters is impartial and as fair as fair can be. Indeed, Mr. Mackiewicz has even been accused of pro-Bolshevism. Still no book on Soviet Russia impresses us more, nor has any made me more keenly conscious of the danger menacing the civilized world.

It is not that the author is blind to the possibilities of failure of Bolshevik plans and undertakings; he shows us impartially the pro and the contra of the whole question, but he does not make the fatal mistake of applying sane criteria to a mad community.

I have over and over again met two mistakes, repeated even by prominent statesmen: one is the tendency to draw a parallel between the Bolshevik nightmare and the great French revolution, the other is the belief that a prosperous Russia under Soviet rule will be much tamer than a starving Bolshevia. After reading *Russian Minds in Fetters*, you plainly see the error of such opinions. I remember in the year 1920 one of the most prominent English statesmen in those days warning Poland not to risk rousing the Bolsheviks, lest a Russian Napoleon should arise in the East and bring confusion to all Europe. If this honourable gentleman, who seemed to fear having to play the part of a modern Pitt, had known something about Soviet Russia, he would rather have spoken of Attila or Gengis-Khan coupled with the efforts of Peter the Great and the fanaticism of the first Mahomedans. This would have been more to the point and quite a different proposition. I really believe that reading this little book might in future save many a mistake and many misconceptions.

I hope *Russian Minds in Fetters* will be read by students of history, philosophy and sociology, and also specially by statesmen. They will all find it useful.

PRINCE EUSTACE SAPIEHA
Former Polish Minister of Foreign Affairs and former Minister of Poland at the Court of St. James

RUSSIAN MINDS IN FETTERS

CHAPTER I

THE CAULDRON STILL BOILS

When I set out from Poland for the Union of Soviet Republics I believed myself to be well equipped for the journey. I had a fairly good knowledge of the history and literature of pre-war Russia, and I had mastered in detail all that had been written about the latest revolution. Furthermore, I had kept in touch with the Soviet Press and literature, and had followed recent happenings in Russia from day to day. Besides also knowing the constitution of the U.S.S.R. almost by heart, I had read the works of Lenin, Trotsky, Lunacharsky, Bucharin and Stalin.

None the less, each day that I spent in Russia broke down some one of the conceptions I had so laboriously built up concerning present conditions in that country. No day passed without revealing or suggesting to me new problems for investigation and solution, new occasions for surprise. Particularly the latter. I felt as though I had been admitted to a garden in which the farther I strolled, the more I was enticed by new walks and views which in their turn revealed other and more distant perspectives.

Soviet Russia provokes continuous astonishment. For instance, a reader unacquainted with the country would find it difficult to believe that this comparison to a garden and its paths would be seriously treated there as "counter-revolutionary," or at least as *petit bourgeois*. Nor would he realize that the books and pamphlets of Bolshevik leaders are no measure of the intensity of the revolutionary feelings prevailing in Bolshevik society, since those leaders belong to the elder generation and, accordingly, do not reflect exactly the predominant attitude of mind at the present time. In her reminiscences, the estimable Mrs. Krupska, who was for many years the wife of Lenin, relates how, a few months before his death, her husband attended a theatrical entertainment given by students. Someone having recited verses of Mayakovsky, Lenin asked for Pushkin. He received the reply: "Pushkin is a bourgeois poet: Mayakovsky is one of us." Lenin smiled and said: "It seems to me that Pushkin is the better."

Without actually having visited Soviet Russia, it is scarcely possible to understand how profoundly that last observation, with its normal estimate of literary values, is out of harmony with the whole atmosphere in which literary criticism exists in that country, where strict Marxian principles are applied to the arts, and where verse and prose, painting and sculpture, stage and screen are all judged primarily from the point of view of the class struggle.

An aim of the present small volume is to raise the curtain on this extraordinary manifestation of corporate existence, the key to an understanding of which is, I believe, afforded by my title, *Russian Minds in Fetters*.

A hint of how little either the works of leading Bolsheviks or the Soviet daily Press can be depended on to give a true picture of conditions and events in Russia was given me on the day of my arrival, when I had an illuminating conversation with a person well acquainted with those conditions. We were talking of the three-volume work, *Vers l'autre flamme*, in which Panait Istrati declares that in Soviet Russia the workmen fare worse than any other class. My interlocutor said that the book in question had no value, and did not give a true picture of conditions in Russia; whereupon I exclaimed that whole chapters of it consisted of extracts from the official Soviet newspapers.

"That does not matter."

"How so?"

"A Soviet newspaper never tells the precise truth. When it does not lie, it exaggerates. If it gives a favourable account of Soviet conditions, it either exaggerates or lies. If the account it gives is unfavourable—for instance, if it says that somewhere or other transport is in a bad way—it is either lying or exaggerating. It goes on the principle that self-criticism must be developed in one direction or another. By publishing an exaggerated description of the neglected state of one branch of work, the Bolshevik leaders hope to increase the energy of those who are employed in that field."

Later on I had repeated opportunities of seeing how well founded is this view that on principle the Soviet Press does not tell the truth and that it cannot therefore be relied upon to give a true picture of things as they are. The ludicrously mistaken notions, for example, concerning Soviet policy in regard to national independence which are prevalent outside the U.S.S.R. can only be explained by the fact that foreign politicians and journalists form their opinions on the strength of what is published in the Soviet Press.

My principal object in visiting Russia was to find answers to five fundamental questions.

1. Whether in the event of a war with one of

her neighbours we might expect to see an outburst of patriotic feeling which would help the Soviet Government in its struggle with a foreign foe, or whether, on the contrary, the outbreak of war would produce a counter-revolution in Russia.

2. On which side the victory will lie in the struggle between Russian-Bolshevik centralism and the decentralizing nationalist forces.

3. What influence Asia exerts on Bolshevik Russia.

4. What a younger generation looks like when it is brought up "without morals" and in the belief that the practice of religion is the pathological symptom of some kind of sexual hysteria.

5. The real interpretation of the Russian "palimpsest." Just as on a palimpsest the half-erased classical Latin characters are recoverable under the prayers which the Middle Ages wrote in their place, so I imagined that in the writings of Soviet men of letters and in films such as those which depict the life of Pushkin or the times of Ivan the Terrible, a certain sympathy and affection, if not a definite longing, for the historic Russian culture might be detected—although, of course, it would be concealed under a superficial communist orthodoxy.

Now that I am home again, I should like to

answer those questions, but at the same time I feel how naïve they were. The very fact that I composed such a questionnaire is evidence of my ignorance of the real conditions prevailing in Soviet Russia. My questions show that I hoped to grasp the static side of Bolshevism, those manifestations of it which would not be liable to great variation. I believed that although, owing to the unfinished state of the five years' plan, the economic situation and the position of the consumer might differ from day to day, none the less those psychological attitudes of the Russian populace which I had framed my questionnaire to elucidate would certainly be settled and definable. In fact, I expected to find in Bolshevik Russia something permanent and unchanging.

I had not in the least realized that contemporary Russia, so far from being a state created by the revolution which has enjoyed, or at least endured, its new constitution for several years past, is to-day a country still in a state of active revolution, a country in which all conceptions and views are still in process of upheaval.

I am not now thinking of executions—which are frequent occurrences—nor even of the struggle with the *kulaks* and *semi-kulaks* which is going on all over agricultural Russia and which affects more people than did the struggle with the Army officers and landed gentry in 1918 and 1919. The revolutionary steam-roller is to-day crushing a far more numerous mass than was the case in the days of militant communism. Nor is the struggle with the *kulaks* and the *semi-kulaks* any more legal or less revolutionary in its character than the massacres of gendarmes and policemen so extensively practised in those years. It was a daily occurrence while I was in Russia, and will no doubt continue to be a daily occurrence, for gangs of rag-tag and bobtail "communists" to set on a *kulak*, rob him of his hay, his cows and his horses, break down his fences and ruin his cottage—after which excesses the Soviet authorities attack the injured *kulak* in their turn and segregate him. The prisons are full of these simple country folk. It is, by the way, the greatest heresy to use the expression "peasant proprietor." There are no peasant proprietors, you will be told indignantly, and only "right-deviators" use such a description. To-day the following terms are applied to country folk and every village is assumed to have some inhabitants in each category: *kulak*, *semi-kulak*, "medium" and "poor." Bolshevik pamphlets sometimes report as an eccentricity testifying to the criminal state of mind in certain rural soviets, that the latter have given in an official return the answer, "we have no *kulaks*"!

But, as I say, to my mind neither the social-revolutionary transformation which is going on throughout the Bolshevik countryside nor its accompanying excesses in the way of robbery, imprisonment, and even bloodshed, afford the most striking evidence that Russia is still at present a great cauldron bubbling over with revolution. Nor am I thinking in particular of that development which was recently so much before the public eye, namely, the wholesale deportation of the population—for instance, of the Polish *petite noblesse*[1] in White Russia to the north, where they work in the forests under compulsion.

The predominant fact is that Soviet citizens are kept in a perpetual state of revolutionary sur-excitation, a mental condition of strife and war with reality, accompanied by all the symptoms usual in such cases—an imperative urge to get rid of as much energy as possible, a feeling of "now or never," a suggestion of hysterical despair in undertaking each new task, etc. It is not only the red placards with their inscriptions hung out

[1] In Polish, *szlachta zagonna*, i.e. persons who, though they possess patents of nobility dating from the times of the old Polish Republic, are and have been for generations past on the same economic level as the mass of the peasants.

in the streets and railway stations, in tramways, in museums and schools, in factories and soup-kitchens, which give expression to these revolutionary incentives. Not until he has acquired a fairly intimate acquaintance with life in Russia can the foreigner realize that, whereas in other countries young people study for the sake of learning and workmen work in order to earn, in Russia the individual is impelled to work not out of regard for his own personal interest, but by two factors of which one is terror. The other is the systematic rousing of the individual into a state of revolutionary hysteria, a condition resembling that of an actor at the moment when he is playing the most emotional of his parts. By daily doses of revolutionary hashish, society is reduced to a condition of chronic hysteria.

Everything in Russia is in a state of flux, everything is relative, everything is carried along on the current of the revolutionary struggle which flows like a river in spate. Later on, I shall show that in the Soviet State no fixed norm of law, either civil, criminal, or constitutional, exists in the European sense of the word "existence." One day it may be declared that the State has nothing to do with the party; on the very next day a financial decree of fundamental importance and with the force of law will be signed by the secretary-general of the party. Every case which comes before the courts, be it civil or criminal, is looked at from the viewpoint of the class struggle. In this amazimg country there is no science, for objectivity in scientific research is prohibited, and all research must be based on the Marxian doctrine.

To look for stable, static elements in the Soviet Russia of to-day is, in fact, much the same as to try to measure with an iron footrule the height of a wooden cottage which is in flames from floor to roof.

Naïve as most of my five questions admittedly are, I shall return to them because, however ridiculous they may seem in Russia, they reflect fairly well the interest which the public of my own country feels in its formidable neighbour. They will help me to find my way through the labyrinth of chaotic impressions, verifications and facts which I brought back with me from Russia. My answers to them will be as short as possible and certainly not exhaustive, but they will form a short introduction to the study of Soviet Russia. The reader will realize that a question which, when posed in Poland, sounds clear, sensible and normal, becomes on Russian territory inconceivably complicated and confused, and can only be answered by a person who has lived through, as it were, an attack of something like insanity.

One important point to begin with. In Poland no normal person believes in a war between that country and Russia—not because he is a pacifist, but simply because he does not believe in it. At first I tried to explain to the Russians I talked with how far removed we are from any thought of aggression. I pointed out to them, for instance—the argument is entirely logical and of capital importance—that the very character of our German policy excluded all possibility of warlike preparations against Russia. Later on I merely shrugged my shoulders.

In Russia every normal person believes in a war. Further, no normal person can understand why Poland or Europe or somebody else has not yet attacked Russia. The failure to do so seems to a Russian so extraordinary that he can only explain it by some perverse cunning on their part. The Bolsheviks reason in this way: "Every year we are becoming more dangerous as an enemy. A few years ago we might have been crushed without trouble. Why do the others not hasten to attack us, seeing that time is working so strongly for us?"

It is quite true that "the danger of aggression by capitalist powers" is necessary to the Bolsheviks as a link in their chain of similar "slogans"—such as the "five years' plan," "collective farms," etc. They are all intended to keep the mass of Russians in a constant nervous state of revolutionary tension and to change the new Russia beyond recognition, so that return to the old scheme of things would be technically impossible. None the less, even if there is some deliberate exaggeration in the emphasis laid on the war peril, and in the dissemination of the idea that Russia is surrounded by enemies, there is a perfectly genuine fear of war—such as might be felt by an enterprising burglar who, having just extracted the money from the safe, is afraid that the police may arrive prematurely.

And here I must profess my entire adherence to the view that Russia is every year becoming a more dangerous enemy. Not because her army is making prodigious progress, especially in technical equipment. Nor because "we have entered on the decisive year of the five years' plan," as to which I have formed a very sceptical opinion.

I have said that the real distinguishing mark of Russia to-day is the state of revolutionary tension in which the country is being constantly maintained. The second factor which is shaping conditions in Bolshevik Russia is the difference of age—of simple, physical age. The difference is incalculable between those who knew the *ancien régime* and those whose childhood fell in the period of the war and whose youth was passed first in the years which witnessed the collapse of Tsardom and later in the confused counter-currents and chaotic war-cries of revolutionary incentives.

As a rule, persons of the former class are hostile to the Soviet system, but, being themselves incapable of action, look to somebody else for salvation; they growl and discharge their impotent irritation in invectives against the *régime* in power.

On the other hand, the younger generation are passionately in love with the Soviet system—a state of mind which a foreigner finds it impossible to understand. Russia, that great, fertile, bounteous country, is starving like a pariah dog. In the streets of Moscow men stand and sell half-chickens, little pieces of sausage and slices—not loaves—of bread. At Nijni-Novgorod, looking out over the magnificently fertile valley of the Volga, I bought a pound of black bread for three roubles, equivalent at the official rate of exchange to about a dollar and a half. A woman teacher, be it remembered, in a primary school, receives eighty roubles (£8 at par) a month! It is impossible to describe the misery in Russia in the matter of dress—the women in Moscow, in Leningrad or Kieff, who walk about in inconceivably rough stockings or in men's slippers with bare calves.

Life is passed in continual, sometimes mile-long queues, whatever the article to be bought. In Leningrad I have seen queues to buy newspapers. How pleasant too are the housing conditions! Each person has the right to six square metres of floor space; and, in the case of divorce, both parties often have to remain in the same room for lack of any other quarters. No one speaks of "our flat"—only of "our room." There is a lack of everything, from swaddling clothes to coffins—not excluding milk and bread, books and medicines. The communal shops in Moscow hire out coffins only for the funeral procession: the corpse is carried to the cemetery—of course, without the assistance of a priest, for that is forbidden—where it is dumped into the grave and the coffin is returned.

But on the background of this nightmare-like daily life there really does exist a younger generation enthusiastically devoted to the Soviet system and in daily expectation of miracles from the five years' plan. Any war or counter-revolutionary movement inside Russia—in the possibility of which latter I do not for the moment believe—would find in this younger generation an obstinate foe, prepared to defend the Soviets with tooth and nail.

The Bolsheviks are well aware of this solidarity which is arising between their system and the young generation. In Moscow there are only young folks to be seen: in the theatres nothing but young faces. At the head of the greatest enterprises and in the most responsible positions young men or girls are to be found. I have seen an officer with a rank corresponding to our full general who did not look as if he were more than twenty-five.

Every intelligent reader will, of course, understand that, if I speak of the difference of age as marking a real distinction, that does not imply that I have not seen children in churches—for which, be it added, they may be dismissed from school—or that I have not met elder persons who are also enthusiasts of the new *régime*. There are exceptions on both sides, but they do not invalidate the rule that the younger generation is for and the older against the Soviets, and that time, by transferring the majority from the latter to the former camp, is the greatest ally of the potential military power of the Soviets.

Men of over thirty, be they peasants, Government officials, or even workmen, usually curse the Soviets and wish them a speedy end. What ought to be called high treason is to be met at every step in Bolshevik Russia. If a cabdriver learns that his fare is a Pole, he generally asks, "When are you coming to deliver us?"

Such is the usual reaction of a peasant if he receives the present of a cigarette. The whole Bolshevik system of terror and the extremely efficient G.P.U. cannot protect the Soviet *régime* from continual questions of that sort. I happened to go into a little country church which had been converted into a soup-kitchen. In Russia it is easy to distinguish foreigners, for only they wear hats and starched collars. About fifty peasants and women were sitting there. One of them made me a little speech, urging me to persuade "my people" to come with an army and help them at last to live like human beings.

It is therefore to be presumed that with the first disasters in the field the Soviet Government would collapse from internal forces, and would no longer have strength to dominate a society which so profoundly detests it. Only I do not know of what the enthusiasm of the Bolshevik youth would not be capable when fired by its first victories. I repeat—so far as prospects of war are concerned, time is the Soviets' greatest ally.

Although I have promised to answer all my five questions, I do not mean to take them in the same order in which I posed them. I should first like to accustom the reader to the psychological atmosphere in which the Bolshevik population lives, for only after he has become familiar with that atmosphere will he be able to understand why the answers fall out as they do, and not otherwise. In Bolshevik Russia one is continually coming across things which seem even more ridiculous than extraordinary. I will start by quoting a few examples, though I am afraid that many readers will take them for jokes or caricatures. They will not believe that such things could be meant seriously. I can assure them they are.

Let me take an example from the exhibition of modern French art in Moscow. In the Kropotkin Street a magnificent museum has been arranged of the works of foreign masters of the latest period, taken from the private houses of wealthy Russians. There are some splendid canvases of Cezanne and Van Gogh, of Renoir and others; in sculpture modern masters, such as Rodin and Bourdelle, are represented. Every little room full of these masterpieces has its placard explaining to visitors the value of the pictures and statuary in it from the viewpoint of Marxian ideology and the class struggle. Thus the art of Picasso is defined in the following terms: "The lower middle-class character of

Picasso undergoes painful adjustments owing to the fact that he is the exponent of those groups of the lower middle-class which are affected by the expansion of industry and thrust themselves into the ranks of the industrial bourgeoisie."

It would be less ridiculous to ascribe satanism to poor Picasso than to inflict on him such a "scientific-economic" interpretation. For us the episode is merely laughable, but it looks more serious when we remember that the thought and culture of what is, after all, a great nation are being throttled by socialist dogma. Let us remember incidentally that the same path is being followed, though less consistently, by socialists all the world over.

In the Ukraine there is an official Bolshevik writer, Comrade Chvylevoy, a member of the party. But he has no luck—he is always writing something which he has to recant later on. Any person who is brought to trial in Bolshevik Russia must, sooner or later, eat humble pie, deny his own convictions, and not only write but also read aloud before the court an "act of contrition" in which he stigmatizes in the most violent terms his own person, his convictions and his life work, and declares explicitly that he has been at fault; he must moreover accuse himself of a number of crimes which he has not committed.

There is something sinister and revolting in these tragi-comic scenes of abasement in which the dignity of a human being is dragged in the mud. Such acts of contrition were pronounced in all cases by the persons who figured in the recent notorious trials—in those of the Society for the Liberation of the Ukraine, in those of Ramzin and his friends of the Industrial Party, and in those of the Mensheviks. Not without astonishment do one's thoughts revert to the "bad old times"—as they were called by a German at Kieff—of the Imperial *régime* when persons were indeed convicted for political crimes, but everyone who took part in the trial, beginning with the public prosecutor, subscribed to the view that a person on trial for his political views must at all events be the hero of an idea.

Comrade Chvylevoy makes one blunder after another, until he finally writes a story called *The Woodcock*, which is declared to be contrary to the doctrine of the party and almost counter-revolutionary! And no wonder, seeing that the story contains such appalling passages as the following:

"The sun set in fiery splendour. His rays sank in the evening waters of Lake Tajtar. The lake, which lay in the middle of the steppe, seemed as silent and solitary, as deserted and helpless as the very idea of separation. From the southern herbage a scent rose and, as always, it was violent and disturbing, suggestive of the scent given off by some fantastic land which was hovering on the edge of the abyss and reflecting profoundly."

I must confess that at first sight I could not detect the counter-revolutionary element in this landscape, which to me in my innocence seemed a very ordinary passage. But if my readers are in the same position, be sure that it is because we are all of us very thickheaded. It is surely as clear as daylight. Russia is in the "decisive year" of the famous five years. All is thunder and expansion as the proletariat intensifies its effort. Huge factories are rising on all sides, the industrialization of the country is forging ahead—and this idiot talks about a pervading quiet and repose, about a fantastic land which is hovering on the edge of the abyss!

As the official and orthodox critic of the unfortunate Chvylevoy, Gortchak writes of this passage with well-merited sarcasm, but also with grief and bitterness that such an improper production should issue from the pen of a comrade and member of the party:

"And this is how Comrade Chvylevoy depicts the general situation of the Soviet Ukraine at the moment when, in an unrivalled effort, it is exerting all its creative forces in the struggle to construct the new edifice of socialism."

Bolshevik men of letters have their own unions, in Russia called R.A.P.P., in the Ukraine U.A.P.P., in White Russia B.A.P.P., and so on. These unions have many members—the R.A.P.P. is said to have ten thousand—but that only means that in them are collected the graphomaniacs from the factories and barns who write on sundry revolutionary subjects. Nothing can occasion surprise in the country in which Demyan Biedny can be treated as a poet merely because he is a workman.

Of course, in such a multitude there are some talents—and even of the first order. But as a matter of fact, the great names of Bolshevism are rather to be found among the publicists. It seems to me that Lenin, with his hammerlike style, was a publicist of the first order. Lunacharsky and Radek are also excellent publicists. I am not surprised that the elements with most artistic value in contemporary Russian literature hold aloof from these crowds of proletarian writers and enrol themselves in the "Union of Soviet Writers." These are the so-called "travelling companions" or "hangers-on." Both term and conception and also the persons so described are at present the subject of very lively discussion in Russia.

The life of such a "hanger-on" is hard. He must write his novel from the first line to the last in such a way as to prove that he is familiar with the doctrine of Marx and also with the conception of the omnipresent class struggle. His subjects are imposed on him. He has to write about the accumulation of grain programme, collective farms, the industrialization of the country, the five years' plan, the Don basin, the new industrial districts in the Urals. There are plenty of subjects, but he must not write about love, or, at any rate, as little as possible; for, in spite of what is said, written and thought about Bolshevik Russia, a real puritanism prevails there. It is forbidden not only to sing but even to play gipsy songs, for it has been recognized that they are sexually exciting, and therefore "bourgeois" in their action.

It must be remembered that the "hanger-on" is entirely dependent on the State, seeing that all the publishing houses are in the latter's hands. The State publishes all books, whether written by a "hanger-on" or by an author from the proletariat, at its own good pleasure, and the edition is as large or as small as it pleases. Nothing else of the country's literary output appears in print, for few writers will try to send their stories to a "counter-revolutionary" publisher abroad. If they were to do so, they would be turned out of their union and, deprived alike of bread cards and of the possibility of employment, would be condemned to starvation. Of late, bitter attacks against these "hangers-on" have appeared in the Soviet Press, not only in political newspapers, but also in those which are devoted to literary and theatrical criticism.

In one of the most authoritative pronouncements the case is put in the following way:—

"We must consider whether the existence of 'hangers-on' is desirable at a time when it has been decided to suppress all retail concerns."

The foreign reader of a novel by one of these writers is likely to assume that he is reading the work of an out-and-out communist. There is so much in the book about the class struggle: so much mud is thrown at the classes which used to be on the top and at the bourgeoisie of Western Europe: Poincaré is described as the slave of the capitalists and Pilsudski as a fascist. But it is of such fiction that the following vigorous and suspicious criticism was offered:—

"Bourgeois literature has been caught in the tongs of the proletariat dictatorship. It only possesses a limited number of lines on which it can attack us: hence it has to wriggle and adapt itself in various ways to existing conditions. None the less, it cannot be pure chance that the quantity of literature of a biographical character has grown enormously of late. Thirteen short stories have been written about Lermontoff alone—among others by writers such as Sergeieff-Ciensky and Boris Pilniak. Nor can it be an accident that some writers show such a predilection for persons of the 'superfluous' class or for problems of a sexual erotic nature. In the last resort such subjects are merely an example in a specialized form of the efforts of the bourgeois ideology to divert the attention of the reader from the class struggle in order to weaken the strength of the proletariat."

Then follows an enumeration of the "hangers-on" and an attack on various passages in their stories which are suspect on the score of bourgeois tendencies, deeply concealed though they may be.

And the conclusion was as follows:—

"In its resolution the Central Committee asked us to be indulgent to the 'hangers-on'. But we have no more need of them: they have given us all they have to give. We have nursed them long enough: all our attention must henceforth be devoted to the literature of the genuine proletarians."

Russia is now in very truth and without any suspicion of bluffing a proletarian state, and the passages quoted above show that in such a state the censorship is far stricter than under any emperors or popes, or in the most rigorous of *Polizeistaaten*. The censorship is no longer merely critical—it even dictates the subject matter. In the proletarian state a writer exists in order to fulfil the state's social commands—in so many words it is laid down. And this happens to the nation which produced Dostoievsky. Before any piece can be acted in public it must be played before workmen from the communist cell in some factory and accepted by them. And this in Russia where the theatre, or rather the theatres, surpass those of Paris in talent, and those of Berlin not only in talent but also in subtlety and charm. In Warsaw we have only great actors, whereas they have both great actors and great theatres. Besides an excellent classical theatre with traditions, they have theatres created by such gifted masters as Stanislavsky, Wachtangoff, Trailoff and Meyerhold. As a matter of fact, I am utterly opposed to Meyerhold, and before I ever knew that he had declared the circus to be infinitely superior to the theatre I said that he had brought the theatre back to the circus and the freak-show. I loathe a theatrical art which consists in searching out a pose for a clown, and which lowers itself to the level of jazz bands and negro orchestras, but I must confess that Meyerhold is a decadent of genius who throws such a light on theatrical problems that his very errors are vivifying. But to-day the Russian theatres must devote the vital energy of their actors and actresses to the attempt —however artistically executed—to suppress free human beings altogether and to substitute for them a collection of human beings welded in a corporate entity by prison discipline. In obedience to Bolshevik puritanism they must help to expel from the theatre—as it has been expelled from art in general—the stimulus of love. The theatres of Russia, as rich in talent as the caps of her ancient princes were in jewels, as intimate and distinctive as the ermine robes of the Romanoffs, have to adapt for the stage the works which peasant writers of the proletariat have scrawled on paper in the clumsy characters of the illiterate. Slavery has never yet existed in a form so utterly opposed to civilization.

And the cinema? Certainly the cinema in Russia is on a level higher than that of the average production in European countries. Unutterably boring, indigestible as the pictures themselves may be, thanks to their revolutionary theme, the technique employed is admirable. Admirable, too, and altogether justified is the conception of the cinema as a separate art dominated neither by actor nor by plot, but by certain artistic conditions inherent in the nature of that great art, the art of the cinema—to wit, movement and light. As a whole, a Soviet film is boring, but in its technique and, in consequence, in such fragments as exhibit the technical skill of the producer, it dazzles and enchants. The art of the cinema, indeed, thrives in an atmosphere of contagious revolutionary hysteria. Being an art of movement, its artistic intensity is frequently proportionate to the intensity with which the impression of movement is conveyed. Finally, the cinema is an art which calls for collective effort. No one man can create a film, for the making of which is required the collaboration of operator and producer, of author, musician and stage manager. The insane efforts of the Bolsheviks to substitute a collective entity for individual human beings find a paradoxical echo in this art. None the less, at the present time the Bolshevik cinema is the scene of a struggle between art for its own sake and art constrained to serve the purpose of propaganda. It has to crawl along under a heavy burden of Bolshevik propaganda, and for this reason the visitor to Russia does not see many really beautiful films—he only feels how fine Russian cinema art might be. It is not the fault of the film director that when, for purposes of propaganda, the cathedral of the Blessed Vassily and a factory chimney are shown side by side on the screen, the artistic merits of the former overshadow those of the latter so that the picture in question is condemned as "unsuccessful." It would be, indeed, a mistake to accept the wonderful propaganda film, "Cruiser Patiomkin," as truly representative of Bolshevik policy in regard to the cinema. Abroad this film has done much to propagate communism, but its culminating moment is undoubtedly the scene in which a child's hand is crushed on the marble stairs under a soldier's heavy boot. And that incident, which rends the heart with its direct appeal to common human sympathies and feelings, has nothing to do with communism, being, in fact, its negation. "You may pass what judgment on us you like from any standpoint but that of humanitarianism," said a Soviet dignitary to me with as much truth as cynicism.

According to the orthodox Bolshevik view, it is erroneous to suppose that anything can be artistically beautiful if it gives expression to tendencies hostile to the proletariat in its struggle with the bourgeoisie. A dramatic piece which glorifies a "bourgeois" fighting against the "people" cannot, they say, be "artistically beautiful." Such a piece, being revolting in its subject, must also be revolting "artistically" and, in consequence, not beautiful. The Bolsheviks shout down the timid voices of the "hangers-on" who would admit that, "though Alexis Tolstoy and Karamzin and Carlyle were enemies of the proletariat, none the less, from the point of view of art, their works possess literary and artistic beauty." Such utterances are regarded as unorthodox, *petit bourgeois*, counter-revolutionary. Similarly, the Bolsheviks entirely condemn the motto of "art for art's sake." According to the Bolshevik ideology artistic values can only be estimated by the amount of profit which a given work of art brings to the cause of the social revolution.

It must be remembered that such profit is not derived exclusively from Bolshevik art. A sensational story which places the life of the bourgeoisie in a luxuriant setting of crime and suspicion, of theft and sexual perversion, may be welcomed by the Bolsheviks even if it was not written by one of them. One of our sentimental or romantic tales in which a girl is seduced by the young squire is a real find for the Bolsheviks, even if written by Stanislas Moniusko, or by a Catholic and conservative such as Lucian Rydel.

It will perhaps be asked how it is possible to express the struggle of Bolsheviks with Mensheviks in an artistic form, or how the problems of politics and economics which fill up everyday life in Soviet Russia can be made the material of artistic expression. The answer is that what in Western Europe is called "private life" is in Bolshevia reduced to almost nothing. Except for the glass of tea which he gulps down every morning after boiling the water on a Primus stove, the individual's existence is controlled by the machinery of public life. His dinner depends on his relation to the Party or on his attitude towards this or that tendency of the highest Soviet authorities. It is easily comprehensible that stories, plays and films should be stuffed with problems drawn from public life. I saw a very powerfully constructed and highly dramatic Bolshevik play called *Bread*. In Moscow it is played in the Stanislavsky Theatre, in Leningrad in the former "Alexander Theatre," in Kieff in the Polish Theatre, where the Orthodox popes who appear in it are transformed into Roman Catholic priests. Among the characters of the play are two communists who have been sent to the countryside to collect grain. One of them behaves badly and unjustly; as might be imagined, he is a secret follower of Trotsky. To start with he yields to the opposition of the villagers and only asks them for four thousand poods of grain instead of the twelve thousand which they ought to furnish. Then, when he receives a card threatening him with death, he loses his temper and demands fifteen thousand instead of twelve thousand poods. How different is the behaviour of his companion, the real, sensible communist! He revokes the demand for fifteen thousand poods, which would look like a forced levy, and asks for twelve—not four—thousand poods, which are to be furnished not by all the inhabitants of the village, but only by the *kulaks*, against whom the poorer peasants are thereby incited. Here in dramatic form is shown the struggle between two Bolshevik types—between the follower of Trotsky, who rushes from one extreme to the other and either capitulates before the villagers, or else imposes on them a forced levy, and his rival, who solves the problem according to the formula of Stalin by creating a line of social cleavage in the village.

CHAPTER II

SEXUAL MORALITY AND EDUCATION

I HAD been trying for two years to obtain a *visa* to visit Russia, when the Soviet Legation in Warsaw finally acceded to my wish with an elegant compliment to the veracity of my journalistic work. "Such a lot of lies are written about us," they said, "but we know that you, monarchist as you are, will only write the truth." I feel myself, in consequence, bound to declare that I shall not set down anything which I did not myself see, and that I was always at pains to check whatever was told me. To quote an instance: I had heard that at present the only source of livelihood of the innumerable Orthodox priests whose churches have been suppressed consists of the fees or alms received for reading the burial service at interments in the cemeteries. The corpse arrives at the cemetery in a coffin hired for its transport only. Passing through the streets the funeral procession has had no religious character whatever, but, if the family is pious, it will ask a priest to celebrate the proper rites over the body, and he, and even the other priests who may be waiting in the cemetery, will receive an alms. Adhering to my principle, I wished to see this with my own eyes before alluding to it in print. I drove to the cemetery indicated, but instead of priests I found on the entrance gate a notice: "Cult workers are strictly forbidden to remain either inside the cemetery or in the streets adjacent to it. Such persons are only allowed to enter and to perform rites individually as required." This prohibition suggested that the unfortunate pauper-popes were to be deprived of their last means of existence, and, as I read it, there rang in my ears words heard at a meeting, "Religion is not persecuted."

It is not my intention to write a work of anti-Bolshevik propaganda. I must repeat once more that I am describing what I have seen with my own eyes and that only after I have set down all my observations and answered my five questions shall I deliver my definitive judgment of Bolshevism and its probable lines of development. At the outset I wish to emphasize my desire for impartiality and to insist that much anti-Bolshevik literature to-day is full of all manner of nonsense. To propagate false accounts of Bolshevik Russia is useless and even harmful. Useless, because no exaggeration is needed to make effective a picture of the nightmare life which exists in Russia. When I left for Russia, my conception of the conditions prevailing there had been formed on the basis of such works of propaganda, but it did not come up to the reality; that is to say, life in Russia seemed to me far worse, far more infernal and intolerable than I had imagined. To render the burden of life in Bolshevik Russia, it is unnecessary to have recourse to exaggeration; it is sufficient to trace in precise and accurate outlines a simple picture of conditions as they are. Exaggeration, rumour and falsehood are harmful because they deform and often diminish the danger which lurks in Bolshevism.

I will begin by giving two examples of the untruths which are often told about Bolshevik Russia. Firstly, we hear of the extraordinary, the inhuman debauchery which reigns there. That is absolutely false. Equally false is the story, cheerfully retailed, that the workmen are exploited by the "commissars"—that the former starve while the latter drink champagne.

The workmen in Russia live worse than their brothers in Poland, not to mention England or Germany. I have satisfied myself that a linotype compositor in Moscow lives on an immeasurably lower scale than a workman of the same class in Wilno. But workmen in Russia live better than other social classes, and are proportionately more privileged than Soviet officials. Whereas, in Poland, the workmen, however well they live, are on the lowest rung of the social ladder, in Soviet Russia the workman, who in what he eats and what he wears, in his lodging as well as in birth, sickness and death is subjected to the nightmare conditions of all existence there, is materially almost and psychologically absolutely on the topmost rung of the ladder in his topsy-turvy country.

But before I proceed to correct mistaken notions about the Bolshevik *régime*, I must point out that the nonsense and the lies the Bolsheviks propagate about foreign countries are beyond all bounds, and can only be described as absurd rather than as monstrous. For instance, in an official publication—but all publications are official—containing character sketches of foreign men of mark, it is said that Pilsudski would probably have been quite willing to serve the Tsar if the latter had not refused to recognize the title of prince to which his family laid claim. At every street corner are to be seen statistical tables proving how terribly badly men live under the capitalist *régime*. The hearts of the Bolsheviks are particularly rejoiced when they read of the number of persons without work in all other countries. But if you tell a young Bolshevik that a man without work in England certainly lives better than a workman who has work in Russia, he will smile and look you in the face with the perfectly sincere conviction that he is talking to a shameless liar.

It is a strange society, hypnotized and united to confront the foreigner with a mendacity so naïve and so disarming as to suggest at times that we really have to do with some kind of mass dementia.

For instance, on one occasion I was travelling in a railway compartment with an elderly engineer who was an enthusiastic admirer of Bolshevism. I put to him the same question as I had put to so many other persons in Russia.

"To what do you attribute the extraordinary disproportion between the figures given by the Bolsheviks themselves of the progress of the five years' plan and the absolute lack of everything in Russia?'

Later on, I heard some interesting explanations on this subject; the engineer, however, surprised me by his reply:—

"The explanation lies in the consumption of our various classes. Before the war, only the socially upper class in Russia was a consumer. Now if you visit the countryside, you will see that our peasant women wear silk stockings."

Now both before and afterwards I visited the countryside in various places, and nowhere, of course, did I see any silk stockings. I did, however, see an actress of the "Little Theatre" with her feet wrapped in rags. Stockings which bear any resemblance to the European article, whether made of silk or not, are a great rarity, an exception, in Russia. Women who are to be seen in the theatres wearing stockings of European appearance, afterwards sit down and pull on shaggy Soviet stockings to preserve such extraordinary possessions from being splashed in the street.

Though no one will maintain that it is an indispensable condition of social happenings for women to be seen in the streets in silk stockings, I do not understand why the Bolsheviks should talk such nonsense on that subject. I once saw a film called "A Relic of the Empire," the plot of which was to the effect that a man who had gone mad during the war only came to his senses in the so-and-so year of the socialist state. He walked through the streets of Leningrad without recognizing the town. Where formerly had been miserable shanties, he saw vast edifices—in which connection it may be remarked, firstly, that the new buildings shown in this film exist not in Leningrad, but in Charkoff; secondly, that, although the Bolsheviks have undoubtedly erected many houses in the workmen's quarter of Leningrad, the centre of the city is conspicuous for its tottering buildings; and thirdly, that nowhere in Russia is to be found a public dressed as are the persons whom the hero of this film sees in the streets and trams. In this particular film, again, all women wear those unfortunate silk stockings.

The longer I sat in that Moscow cinema the more amazed I was. Surely the other spectators knew the conditions of their own life sufficiently well to realize that the picture on the screen was almost humorous in its unlikeness to the truth? Were both they and the authors of the film victims of an hypnotic influence?

I must, however, return to my task of correcting mistaken ideas of Bolshevia, and I shall begin by saying that, in my opinion, it is at least a gross exaggeration to suggest that sexual debauchery is rampant in Russia. It is true that the law hardly puts any limits to divorce, which is in consequence much more frequent than in other countries. It happens too, as I have said, that a divorced couple may continue to live in the same room, for the reason that under the law in force a single person is only entitled to six square metres of living-room floor space—in some towns to more—and it is difficult to find a new lodging. The question of alimony is dealt with very strictly, and a woman has the right to claim alimony even if she does not herself know who is the father of her child.

It should be pointed out that the Bolshevik propaganda, for instance in theatre and cinema, is most explicitly directed against frequent divorce. Men and women who often divorce are laughed at and made ridiculous, like the workers of either sex who are always wanting to change their factory. In the film which I have just mentioned, the workman who recovers his senses after years of insanity finds his wife married to another man. The new husband behaves badly to her and beats her. She is still in love with her former husband, but he refuses to violate the principle of Soviet marriage by taking her back. When he sees his former wife ill-treated by her new husband, he begins by clenching his fists; then the vision of "regeneration by socialism" rises before him and he turns to his work with a sigh, but with eyes serene.

In this film marriage is treated on almost Catholic lines as a union not to be broken even if it becomes burdensome. Although I do not in the least wish to maintain that a film of this sort will stop a quarrelsome couple from going to the registrar and having their divorce entered in the records, it is, I think, interesting that the ideology of Bolshevik Russia, unlike that of Kemalist Turkey, does not at all encourage divorce.

The question of procuring abortion has found a radical solution, and on this point there is a great difference between Bolshevik and Catholic moral principles. In comparing Bolshevik society with any other society we must, however, remember that, whereas the attitude of the Roman Catholic Church in matters of sexual morality is dogmatically logical and clear, the same cannot be said of the Protestant bodies, including the Anglican Church. Not here, therefore, are we to seek for the mark distinguishing our world from that of the Bolsheviks. Further, when we speak of abortion, it is well not to raise our voices too much lest the Gospel words about the Pharisees be quoted against us.

Debauchery, in the real sense of the word, means looseness of life, sexual excesses and the like. Now there is no prostitution in Russia. It may perhaps still lurk in some dark corners, but there is certainly no open and visible prostitution such as exists not only in Paris, Berlin and Warsaw, but also in London. Moreover, the whole machinery of the State is used to combat all sex appeal. Moscow possesses a music-hall, but its ballet dancers are clothed from head to foot. I have already mentioned that the singing and playing of gipsy songs and music has been prohibited on the ground that they are sexually exciting. And although youthful communists are allowed to indulge in respectable dances, the steps which are in vogue at balls given by our own good society are in Soviet Russia regarded as on a level with prostitution.

As for the facility with which, it is alleged, sexual relations are established, I cannot see why it should be greater in Bolshevia than in Europe. On the contrary, the general poverty and misery, the perpetual standing about in sometimes mile-long queues to obtain anything, the insufficient nourishment, all militate against any exuberance of eroticism.

I should like to deal with this subject thoroughly and to devote more consideration to the "puritan" tendency, to which I have alluded above, of Bolshevik ideology in sexual matters. Bolshevik Russia is fond of portraying Europe in the *négligé* of a cocotte. Panait Istrati, who is really a communist, has written three volumes of anti-Soviet propaganda, and, although the communists call him a calumniator, he maintains that he prefers the Soviet to the bourgeois world, and illustrates the grounds for his preference by describing the spectacle of a woman and a dog which he was shown in a Paris brothel.

Here, too, are some quotations from the works of Lunacharsky, one of the most talented representatives of Bolshevik thought:—

"Nowhere better than in a ballroom can you see the bourgeois world with the mask off—the lifeless, wooden rhythm of the jazz band, the screechings of the saxophones, the jerks and skips, the indecent quiverings of densely packed crowds, where no one ever laughs simply, naturally and decently like a human being. The women are painted and their faces are like coloured masks. You might think that all these men and women have been hired to knead dough with their feet. Their activities are presided over by a monkey-like negro, at a sign from whom the whole herd stands still or begins again to hop and skip. And if, after attending such a ball given by the Satan of capitalism, you walk out into the street, the same spectacle will meet you everywhere. These people have had their souls torn out, and there is in them no longer any certainty of the morrow. The fox-trot has burrowed deep into their nerves and muscles."

In his desire to make the capitalist world repulsive, Lunacharsky so far forgets himself as to use the expressions "soul" and "Satan," but if we read this passage of the Bolshevik leader word by word, we must admit with something like panic that it calls up very unexpected reminiscences of *Quo Vadis?* Anyone who has spent some time in Bolshevia must confess that aversion to the capitalist world is bound up with and takes in part the form of aversion to its sexual and erotic licentiousness.

Let us close our eyes and visualize Pompeii, that wonderful specimen of a civilization developed to the point of satiety, of superb wealth and alarming prosperity. We can never recall Pompeii to our minds without thinking of its moral corruption, of its employment in every house of certain organs of the human body as a decorative motive in frescoes and friezes, as a symbol of good luck on the outside of houses, as a knick-knack or as a jewelled trifle to hang on a woman's neck. On the background of that prosperity and that high intellectual culture arose Christianity, with its loathing and contempt for moral corruption. To compare Bolshevism and Christianity is for us sacrilege, and for the Bolsheviks impudent calumniation. It is a comparison of the heights of spirituality with the depths of materialism, of the spirit with the materialist doctrine of Marx. I shall return to this subject; indeed, I must do so, for it is this gulf fixed between the Christian cross and the Bolshevik star which forms the central point of the real ideological struggle between us and them. For the moment, however, I merely wish to establish the analogy that, just as the ancient world connected riches with moral corruption, so to-day the apostles of Bolshevism attack bourgeois civilization by means of pictures of its sexual libertinage.

I have already said that workmen in Bolshevia form a privileged social class. If it be asked who goes to universities, technical schools, polytechnics and other centres of higher education, the answer is that they are thronged by workmen and women, and, what is more, by persons who merit that description, not merely because their parents belonged to the working class, but because they themselves are workpeople in the literal sense of the word.

A person who has spent seven years at a school and finished the supplementary three years' course at a *Technicum* is not usually sent on to an institution of university rank, *Wuz* or *Wtuz*. The *Technicum* is a professional school—there are such institutions for pedagogics, for agriculture, etc. The universities and polytechnics, on the other hand, are open in the first instance to workmen who have hitherto been working in a factory and who pass straight from it to the university.

As regards their preparation for higher studies,

they may have completed a *Rabfak* or course at an evening school for workmen, or have taken some correspondence courses. The first months at the university are, it was explained to me, devoted to giving the students an introduction to higher learning and to filling up the gaps in their knowledge.

To us, all this seems like a story out of the *Arabian Nights*, and I shall therefore give a practical example of the results. While in Moscow I paid a visit to what used to be the Don Monastery. The cemetery attached to the monastery, in which are buried many of the noblemen and wealthy merchants of Moscow, has been "purified": that is to say, most of the monuments have been destroyed and thrown away, and only a few allowed to remain. The monks have been dispersed, and the monastery now houses part of the old Rumianceff Museum and—an anti-religious museum. There are some old furniture and a few pictures of the German, Flemish and Italian schools. The museum was shut when I arrived. After strolling about under the trees, which were just bursting into bud, and deciphering the titles of princes on their ruined tombs, I proceeded to the office of the director, to whom I introduced myself as a foreign journalist. In Russia everyone is very polite to a foreigner, and in all my wanderings through towns and villages I have never had any unpleasant experience. On the present occasion the director, who was a simple workman, was quite ready to show me his museum.

I realized at once that, like a machine which has been wound up, he was repeating to me the same arguments against religion which I had heard in other anti-religious museums. But he retailed them so naïvely that it is worth repeating our conversation.

Standing in front of two pictures from the former Rumianceff gallery, he said:—

"It is said that once upon a time there lived a certain St. John. The best proofs that there never was such a saint is that we have two pictures of him, on one of which he is represented without and on the other with a beard."

"Perhaps he had shaved off his beard," I observed timidly.

"Nonsense—besides, comrade, you see that the faces are quite different."

Further on, we halted again before a picture of the Flemish school depicting the Holy Family.

"You see, comrade, to begin with the bourgeois pretended that Jesus Christ, who, according to them, existed, was a proletarian and so they put him in the hay. Later on, they wanted to make him one of themselves, so in this picture you see the so-called Holy Family in typically bourgeois surroundings. The Virgin Mary looks like a fat bourgeois and Jesus like the well-fed child of a bourgeois family. Everything is arranged about them with bourgeois comfort, and even the cat is mewing."

Finally we came to the main church of the monastery. A malicious mockery had confounded in one heap utensils of the Christian liturgy and objects used in synagogues and mosques. On the top of a chalice lay a black-and-white Jewish praying-shawl; behind the iconostasis part of the altar supported the model of a Mahomedan mosque. We passed in front of one of the greatest treasures of the Orthodox world, the miraculous picture of Our Lady of the Don—to-day no more than another exhibit in an anti-religious museum.

Onwards, onwards—we shall return again to this place and to these problems which hurt and humiliate.

The director is leading us to another building where he will show us that the Imperial Government "even went so far" as to decorate Jesus Christ with its own orders. I bent down to examine the officer's cross of St. George which hung beneath the crucifix. The inscription on the copper plate said that a bullet had hit the cross and that in this way a colonel whose name I did not note had escaped death.

After showing me on the way "a half-naked woman of the nobility"—which turned out to be the monument of a Princess Troubetskoi in the pseudo-classical style of the first decade of the nineteenth century—the director of the museum gave an explanation of an engraving which hung on the wall.

"That is the Russian eagle, the imperial eagle, pecking and tearing the French white eagle."

The "French white eagle" was, of course, the White Eagle of Poland; the engraving dated from 1863, and by the side were printed patriotic verses in Polish.

Being already accustomed to explanations of this kind, I was enduring with patience the entertaining lesson of the director of the museum, when something in our conversation revealed to me that I was in the company of a student who had completed the courses of the historical faculty of the Moscow University.

The reader will now understand why I have been at pains to quote all the nonsense which my companion told me. I wished to show the intellectual level of a man who had studied history at a university and was unable to distinguish between French and Polish. At the moment when I talked to him he was just taking an examination. He had already successfully passed all except two for which he was then cramming. Reluctantly I began to talk to him about history. The Bolsheviks have their own way of teaching history without giving any historical information. They jettison practically all the subject matter of that science and divide the past into periods according to the strict theory of Marx, on the basis of the class struggle and the persecution of the working class. In a word, their history is simply socialist rubbish, but even within those limits my learned friend floundered hopelessly. Not that I found him repulsive. On the contrary—his eyes were aglow with love of learning. He told me how difficult he had found it at first to study, and how glad he was that he had a position in his own special branch of science. As a matter of fact, the honest fool's real profession was joinering. He had, however, passed the war in the ranks of the Red Army and had afterwards worked in a factory, whence his colleagues had sent him to the university—where he had now completed his higher historical studies.

Later on, I saw enough to convince myself that the worthy man whom I have just described was, even if not absolutely typical, certainly not in any way exceptional. Courses of higher study are attended by men with entirely undeveloped intellects who, just because they belong to the working class, are supported and helped and personally conducted through their examinations. In a play called *The Stars are Shining*, which I saw at a theatre, a professor who is examining candidates for the university, asks for the meaning of the term "revolution"; no one can reply, until at last a girl says: "It is when the proletariat does that to the bourgeoisie"—and she made the motion of slitting a throat. On the strength of this one answer the professor admitted "all the candidates to the university." I thought at first that the scene was mere theatrical symbolism; as a matter of fact, it is a realistic picture.

Just because he is what he is, a workman—provided, of course, that he is duly guaranteed by his comrades in the factory—can not only enter the university, but be accepted into the first category of students. For the same reason, he can be sure of taking his degree.

From Moscow to Djerjinsk I travelled in a first-class compartment with an elderly engineer who remembered the Imperial *régime*, and who was also professor in a higher technical school. He was an enthusiastic admirer of Bolshevism.

Remembering my conversation with the museum director, I remarked:—

"I can understand that it is possible without much difficulty to lecture on jurisprudence or history, but how can you teach technical subjects to persons who are so little prepared?"

For my own part, I felt that, however unimportant it might be that tourists should be shown over a museum by an idiot, I should not like to cross a bridge built by such a man.

"Yes," said the engineer, "it is a fact that after they have finished their courses at the *Wtuz* some of our pupils cannot write correctly, even according to our simplified orthography. But they are engineers all the same—something in the style of American engineers. We go in very much for specialization."

"And how they control us," he added, with delight in his eyes. "How they follow every word to be certain that it is above suspicion, and that we are teaching them properly and not ourselves getting into a muddle."

There are practically no real lectures at Russian universities, where the work is more on the lines of a conversation between professor and students. I attended some law lectures at the Moscow University, where I did in fact notice the suspiciousness of the students lest the professor should "distort" some fact.

The Soviets already have plenty of "red"

professors—mainly men who completed their university studies before or during the war. I was told that excellent scientific work is being done in Russia, and science is certainly well endowed there. Nor do I wish to assert that all the students, even of the working class, who pass through the universities are of as low an intellectual level as the example I have quoted. It must be remembered that it is the man who has come to the front who goes to the university. Hence it is not surprising that in Bolshevia there should be some phenomenal intelligences among the workmen, who are favoured in every respect. I made the acquaintance of one uneducated workman—an out-and-out Bolshevik—who impressed me by his intelligence and his knowledge in all fields, as well as by the sober and liberal manner in which he conducted the discussion. He was the president of the trade union of transport workers. None the less, after making all these reservations, and allowing most fully for all the possibilities which the Bolshevik system of higher education furnishes, I hold that, in the last resort, we must consider that system to be what it looks at first sight—namely, nonsense.

In order to glorify the results of the system, an enormous amount of *blague* is employed—of that *blague* in the repetition and dissemination of which, as I have already observed, all that section of the populace which believes in Bolshevism—I use the term advisedly—is united. I was told that in the dockyard at Leningrad are confined four hundred newly-baked Soviet engineers who wander idly from room to room because they are too incompetent to be entrusted with any work. I did not verify this story, but it seems to me very plausible; I can, however, give details of another case in which I caught an eminent representative of Soviet science indulging in *blague*.

In the search for answers to my second and third questions—policy regarding nationality and Asia—I naturally had recourse to the Eastern Institute in Leningrad, which has arisen out of the former Imperial Institute for Oriental Languages. I made the acquaintance of Professor Vorobieff, its director, a courteous and intelligent scientist, who entertained me to tea and gave me an extremely interesting account of his institute. Some of the pupils come from China and India, from beyond the limits of Bolshevia, but there are also plenty of Russians trying to acquire a knowledge of various parts of Asia. In order, however, to be accepted, would-be pupils from the Asiatic provinces must belong to the poorest classes. A "bey" from Central Asia, who is more or less equivalent to our gentleman farmer, could never enter the Institute. Personally, I take an enthusiastic interest in Asia. Whenever I think about that continent my imagination carries me away. When, therefore, I heard from Professor Vorobieff that his Institute has three departments —philology, sociology and economics—I immediately asked him if he did not think that, in considering a problem such as the future of the Asiatic continent, the sciences which go to make up geography are extremely useful. In order to make my point clearer, I suggested that new deposits of gold might be discovered in some little explored district of northern Asia. Such a discovery would greatly influence the movement of population in a given direction. Hence the problems of geographical science must be taken into serious account so far as the future of Asia is concerned. Should they not also be studied in the Institute?

"No," replied Professor Vorobieff, "for my Institute only deals with the peoples of southern Asia, with countries which are already settled and sometimes even over-populated. The problems in which you are interested are studied by another institute—that of the Peoples of the North. There they do in fact deal with the Asia of countless possibilities, and there you will find the students working at geographical problems."

"But in that case the students must be Russians?"

"Certainly not. The institute has a four years' course, and only those candidates are accepted who belong to races living on the fringe of the Arctic Circle. At the present moment twenty-six nationalities from the north of our territory are represented there."

"But all those Aleutians, Tunguses, Jakuts and Samoyedes are savages. Surely such a man brought straight from his hut cannot mature sufficiently in four years to be able to solve scientific problems such as those I mentioned?"

"He most certainly can."

"I should like to see with my own eyes."

Professor Vorobieff at once set to work to obtain for me permission to visit the Institute of the Peoples of the North, but he could do nothing by telephone. It was the eve of the First of May, and at the moment there was nobody in the institute; neither rector nor vice-rector nor professor—not a soul of any sort, in fact. Such, at any rate, was the account which his secretary gave me.

I greatly regretted this failure, for I was very anxious to see scientists from the Polar regions. Trusting to luck, however, in spite of the answer I had received that there was "nothing to be done," and without taking anyone into my confidence, I drove to the Institute of the Peoples of the North, where I was taken for a foreigner who had come to Leningrad for the First of May festivities. I had no time to dispel these illusions, for I was too much interested in the types of both men and women I saw there. They were all creatures of small stature whom Zagloba[1] would certainly have had smoked and then taken home to hang up as votive offerings in the parish church at Lowicz. They were yellow-skinned and almond-eyed, with thick lips, square heads, and crooked feet. The women wore stockings, and the men, too, were dressed to resemble normal Soviet citizens. There were about 260 of them in all—rather grotesque specimens physically, but they received me with the greatest cordiality. I do not in the least deny that, when they return to their huts in the Far North, these men and women will be of immense importance to the Soviets as apostles of the Bolshevik catechism, but so far as their ability to solve geographical problems is concerned, I can only say that the third-year students could not express themselves in Russian without difficulty, while those who were in their fourth year were far from being

[1] Zagloba is a character in the Trilogy of Sienkiewicz—a typical Polish country gentleman of the seventeenth century.

adepts in the four elementary rules of arithmetic.

The conviction that a workman, just because he is a workman, has capacity in every direction, seems to have become a dogma in Soviet Russia. In the *Woks*, or "Inter-Soviet Society for Cultural Intercourse with Foreign Countries," I had the pleasure of talking to Professor Borozdin, who is an expert on questions of nationality. He dictated to me a list of books, which I noted down. By his side was sitting a workman who had been specially delegated to deal with Poland, Latvia, Estonia and Finland. I do not know why, for he did not speak the languages of any of those countries, and he had no idea whatever of conditions in them. Before the war he had worked in the Lapin printing works at Moscow. While Professor Borozdin dictated to me his bibliography, this "comrade" interrupted with the titles of pamphlets which happened to come into his head. They did not in the least conform to the character of the literature which Professor Borozdin was indicating for my use, but the latter none the less hastened to accept every suggestion with a prompt and ready submission to the opinion of the workman, which was very obvious. This dogma of the superiority of the workman in every field is unspeakably stupid and ridiculous.

CHAPTER III

DAILY LIFE IN BOLSHEVIA

In order to complete my sketch of the background on which will emerge the answers to the questions which tormented me, I must gather up in one section a good deal of scattered information about the daily life of an average man in Russia. To some extent I shall repeat what is generally known, and sometimes even what I have myself written elsewhere; otherwise, the picture would not be comprehensive.

In the life of the family the private kitchen plays no part. The children eat in their schools, the parents in their factories. In Leningrad I was shown a factory kitchen which provided sixty thousand dinners. The meals are given out to be eaten elsewhere, with the exception of twelve thousand dinners and suppers, which are consumed on the spot by workmen from neighbouring factories. The queues of persons waiting for these dinners were enormous. It was six o'clock when I visited the soup-kitchen; the doors were closed, but through their glass panes I could see a number of persons whose turn had not come that day. Only workmen are allowed to eat in that immense soup-kitchen. The food was very much like what my generation of students ate in Warsaw in the winter of 1916 to 1917 during the German occupation. On the day of my visit there was soup, meat with grated potatoes, and some sort of sweet made of flour. None the less, that particular soup-kitchen was regarded as a model and was shown with pride.

Everywhere an effort is made to give something better to workmen than to other classes of society. The members of the editorial staff of the *Izvestia* regard it as an honour that they are allowed to eat and enjoy a common table with the workmen engaged in printing that newspaper.

In the schools children are not all fed alike; poor children are given more to eat.

Soviet ideology is directed towards the creation of a collective human unit and the destruction of individualism in life with its tendencies to comfort, to cleanliness and tidiness, to seclusion in the quiet of the home—perverted notions which could only be born in a bourgeois brain. One of the most revolting reminiscences which I carried away from Bolshevia was the description in a book by Mrs. Krupska, Lenin's wife, of the mode of life of Vera Zasulitch, who shot at a governor and was acquitted by the Russian court

—in the bad old times of imperial tyranny, when such occurrences were possible, which is certainly not the case nowadays. Living abroad, Vera Zasulitch kept her room in a state of extraordinary untidiness, which offended Mrs. Krupska—and the latter has my sympathy. Vera Zasulitch had no fixed times for meals; when her stomach called for nourishment, she cooked on a Primus stove a piece of meat which she afterwards cut up with her scissors and ate. I must confess that to me this picture of a woman hacking her fried meat with a pair of scissors is more repugnant than anything else in Bolshevik ideology.

In Minsk a new model house has been built for workmen with clubrooms and reading-rooms and bathrooms and everything conceivable. In it families of the working class have, it is true, separate bedrooms, but so arranged that the door from the passage leads not into one but into two rooms. Hence the inhabitants do not really live in a room of their own, but in a sort of passage. No family can have a home of its own, but must always suffer an intrusion of some sort. In this way the individual is introduced to life in a collective unit.

To state the position epigrammatically: The Tsar shut up a fractional percentage of the whole population in the collectivism of prison life; the Bolsheviks are thus imprisoning the whole population.

After I had already published ten of the articles which make up this book, I was asked by a couple who own a house in Russia whether they could sell it and take the money out of the country. I must own that the inquiry depressed me by making me feel that my articles had not given any impression of what is happening in Russia. The period of the "N.E.P." ("New Economic Policy") is long past and dwelling-houses are now administered in various ways; but there is no such thing as private property in houses. Even if small suburban houses in need of repairs are sometimes let to a private contractor, the latter is not in any way an owner.

Further, there is neither private trade nor private industry nor private handicraft. The concessions which were formerly granted by the Soviets to foreign capitalists have been wound up, redeemed, or made the subject of chicanery. The private trade which was permitted by the "N.E.P." and which supplied Russia with everything in fairly large quantities has been "liquidated" almost entirely by the imposition of very high taxation. The co-operatives, "ARTIELS" as they are called, pay less in the way of taxes, but of late they, too, are being persecuted out of existence. This is particularly true of those co-operatives which are suspected of being merely an association of a few private persons.

The only private businesses which can be said to exist at the present time in Soviet Russia are those of such extremely small "capitalists" as cabdrivers and craftsmen who mend galoshes, Primus stoves and the like. But even they are mercilessly harried. Before the war there used to be six thousand cabdrivers in Moscow; now there are only six hundred, each of whom has to pay annually two thousand roubles (£200 at par) in taxes. At the time of my visit a pood—sixteen kilograms—of oats cost twenty-five, and a pood of hay twenty-six roubles, which, at the official rate of exchange, was equivalent to thirteen United States dollars (£2 12s. at par).

All workmen and officials, all members of unions, are assigned to a "close distribution centre," that is to say, to a shop which should distribute all manner of articles. To the question whether those shops can in fact provide the public with what they require, I can best reply by describing some scenes which I witnessed with my own eyes.

Not long ago were opened some shops "based on commercial principles"—which sold, that is to say, to all customers. Let us imagine a shop of the dimensions of a fair-sized general supply store with several floors. The crowd which throngs it is as thick as in a Catholic church on Easter Eve. There is no room in it for the proverbial pin. What has happened? A rumour has got abroad that somewhere on the third floor of the shop women's boots, size 40, are for sale, and the whole crowd, numbering perhaps over ten thousand persons, has collected in a dense queue several kilometres in length in order to fight its way to those boots which, be it observed, are being sold at a high price.

The reader is perhaps curious as to what happens on the other floors of the big shop, seeing that the stock is exposed for sale on the topmost. Nothing happens on them, and there is no stock. I have seen one shop of very considerable dimensions the entire stock of which consisted of three—literally three—lady's snowboots—one pair and an odd boot.

The crowd which throngs and presses to buy boots is not by any means composed of rich foreigners; it is the ordinary Soviet crowd, composed partly of workmen and partly of peasants; the women wear shawls over their heads and the faces are "communal," as the description ran in 1840. Such a crowd would certainly have co-operative stores of its own, and the fact that it squeezes and pushes and stands in queues for hours is a sufficient proof that those co-operatives are a failure.

In Moscow there are some shops nicknamed "museum-stores" and intended to impress foreigners, at which butter, sausages, caviar, wine, smoked fish, etc., are sold at high prices. Those shops are thronged with just the same working-class public, prepared to spend its last coppers on buying a little butter or a scrap of sausage. I do not think that that would happen if the co-operative stores disposed of an abundant stock.

As I travelled down the Volga during the spring floods with so many visions and apparitions of the past before my eyes, churches on the hill-tops and monasteries buried in orchards, I made the acquaintance of a woman teacher from Samara, an out-and-out Bolshevik and a member of the Union of Communist Youth. A corner of her chemise, which was visible in the opening of her blouse, prompted a question:

"What do you do," I asked, "if you want to buy a chemise?"

"They gave us cards in January," she replied, "but at that time I had no money."

"And when you do buy, do you buy a chemise which you like, or just what they give you?"

"What they give me, of course."

Then she added:

"Sometimes it is hard, very hard, that there should be nothing, but then I remember that there is so much work to be done, and that the structure of socialism is arising."

"The structure of socialism" is a clumsy but a literal rendering of the Russian words which are to be heard at every step.

I arrived at Nijni Novgorod in the morning and learnt that there would be no restaurant on the boat by which I was to travel down the Volga; I should be able to get hot water to make tea, but everything else I must provide myself. At the head of a small detachment, I set out for the town in search of provisions. In my hunt for glasses for tea I went into a Government shop. It was a building with several floors, and I found in it neither more nor less but literally the following objects: four glass vases for fruit, from forty to fifty small statuettes, and from five hundred to a thousand little chairs on wheels for babies.

In the provision shops of Nijni Novgorod I found two uncooked hams. There were also fifty or more boxes, all of the same type, standing on the shelves; I am very sorry that I did not ask what was in them.

Once more I must emphasize the fact that

these were very large shops of several storeys each.

In my hunt for glasses I was taken to a second-hand shop which dealt in old-fashioned mahogany furniture, marble figures, pictures and arms. It, too, was packed to its utmost capacity with the same working-class public, which was fighting for chipped cups of old earthenware in order to drink its tea, and even bought old-fashioned cutlery with the cracked china in order to have knives and forks.

Although I was in the company of two persons who knew the town, I trudged up and down Nijni Novgorod from ten in the morning until four in the afternoon without being able to buy a glass. However, I was able to buy a teaspoon from an acquaintance of one of my porters.

What impressed me in Bolshevia was the contempt for the consumer. In Poland it is the normal thing for a representative of the workmen to declare in the Diet that "the workmen have nothing to eat," or for a representative of the peasants to wax lyrical over the desperate state of his fellows. In Russia that would be inconceivable. Neither at a meeting of the "C.I.K." nor elsewhere could any person present possibly complain that this or that class of the population was starving, had nothing to eat, or was in a poor way. The impression such an action would arouse there can only be compared to the sensation which would be created in a European Parliament if a member, after obtaining the permission of the Speaker, were to declare with pain-contorted countenance, "Honourable members, I have got a terrible stomache-ache." Painful as stomach-ache no doubt is, and however much sympathy and compassion a sufferer from it may deserve, laughter would be the lot of anyone who made a speech of that sort. The example is a very good one, for in just that way are all unpleasantnesses arising out of the domination of the socialist system treated in Bolshevia. Someone is starving —well, let him die. What does it matter to anyone else? In Russia there is no trace of our humanitarianism based on the conviction that, if somebody is starving, the rest of humanity has no more pressing or noteworthy duty than to run and lavish good food on him. But in Russia, if you are hungry, you can die. It is a splendid solution of the problem.

After leaving Russia, I read a report by one of the leading Polish industrialists of his impressions of Bolshevia. In words which were so cautious as to be perhaps a little colourless, he expressed the opinion that what most of all strikes and amazes all foreigners in Russia who understand the language of the country is the cult of work, the attitude of worship towards it and the intoxication with its slogans. The sole aim of man's existence is to work, work, work. Whenever any casual travelling companion asked me what I liked best in Russia, I was able to reply with complete sincerity:—

"The fact that you all talk about work."

In other countries travellers in railway trains talk about notorious cases in the law courts, about the rise of prices and the reduction of salaries, about Cabinet Ministers and watering-places at which to spend the holidays. In Russia they discuss where a factory is to be built and what sort of a factory it will be. Our world is a holiday world, which amuses itself with politics and tennis, which lives on both bread and culture. Theirs is a world of hysteria and exclamatory slogans, of wrestling with work. I must underline this last phrase, for although I do not believe in the results of that work, an hysterical cult of it does, I repeat, undoubtedly exist.

The five years' plan—let us make use of the expression, although the plan in question cannot be seriously said to live up to its name—is just another expression of that contempt for the consumer. I have already mentioned that at first I used to put to all persons one of those naïve and stupid questions such as are asked in dozens by all foreigners in Bolshevia, until they realize that in such a topsy-turvy world and among a nation which has gone mad, normal questions sound as ridiculous as the famous "what does the crocodile eat for breakfast?" in Kipling's charming fable of the baby elephant. The particular question of mine which I have in mind concerned the proportion between the "achievements" of the five years' plan and the present state of the market. The five years' plan does not take the consumer into consideration, and its immediate object is not in the least to diminish the shortage of goods in Russia.

The five years' plan really means the industrialisation of Russia. I know that it has its tradition in the history of Imperial Russia, and that Wyshniegradski, the predecessor of Witte in the Ministry of Finance, used the very slogan—"We may be hungry, but we are exporting"—with which we now reproach the Bolsheviks. It is a known fact that Wyshniegradski's successors were just as forcible in their support of Russian industry and that they derived the funds for that support from taxes which pressed hardly on the peasants. History repeats itself. All this seemed to me very important and real when I set out for Russia. Nowadays such thoughts make me smile, just as do the superfluous scientific trimmings used to trick out the discussion of Bolshevik problems.

The emphasis in the five years' plan is laid on the heavy industry. Bolshevik Russia wishes to prepare herself for the work of production, and the object of the five years' plan is to furnish her, not with goods, but only with factories and machinery for the production of goods. The light industries are treated as a mere means to that end. They also are not run, in the first instance, in the interest of the consumer. The Bolsheviks try to export the products of the light industries in order to receive for them dollars, and in exchange for those dollars machinery. Such is the framework of the five years' plan.

The workman in Russia cannot escape from propaganda or close his ears to politics. Every day he is torn from his work in order to take part in the obligatory chat on subjects taken from the politics of the day. Not to mention that his head is packed with this propaganda in every house and at every street-corner with its inevitable loud-speaker. One of the methods which suits the dominant tendency to spread hysteria among the entire population is the so-called "socialist rivalry." The feeling of rivalry which affects groups and collective units, and may be exploited for utilitarian purposes, the Bolsheviks have turned into a regular system. At the beginning of each year they submit the economic plan to the workmen for acceptance, and they encourage the various departments in a factory to compete as to which can accomplish the most.

And that is as much as can be said in praise of the Bolsheviks—the fact that they work. In my opinion their work will not have any results, and it is therefore a matter of little importance whether they are really working or are only talking about it, whether their statistics are correct or are, to use a phrase of Disraeli, merely one of the forms of lying.

I am not an economist, but I am sometimes inclined to think that, if I had the brilliant talent of Bernard Shaw, I should make fun, not so much of doctors, as of economists. I should write a play in which the economists made all the same prophecies as they made before the war and have been making since. In it those prophecies would find just the same confirmation as they have found in reality, and one of the characters of a dialectical turn of mind would maintain the thesis that, in spite of great names and great authority, economics as a science is still in swaddling clothes—in the same stage as medicine two hundred years ago. Of course, one would need the talent of Shaw in order to say such things publicly; I realize that fact, and have therefore chosen the cautious and cowardly path of description.

My conclusions are as follows: the Bolsheviks are suffering from a lack of goods, which lack, according to them, proceeds from the fact that Russian industry has not yet been sufficiently developed to meet the needs of the internal market, while they will not and cannot purchase goods from capitalist countries. Let us suppose for the moment that their explanation is sound up to this point; but if so, what is happening to agriculture and the production of foodstuffs?

Formerly Russia exported foodstuffs, and yet the population ate well. The statistics hurled about by the Bolsheviks are as dazzling in this as in other fields. It is said that the "*Sowchoz-Gigant*" in Kuban produces by itself one hundred and six million poods of grain. Why, then, is there famine in Russia? Why is it that in the streets of Moscow bread is sold by the crumb, that in Nijni Novgorod a pound of bread costs three roubles, that Russia, the granary of the world, is as hungry as a starving dog?

Let us put the matter in another form. Suppose that a traveller enters the refreshment room at a railway station. He is offered a plate of thin soup made of greens which, outside Russia, no dog would touch. But if he goes to the back of the station building he will find there countrywomen—one with milk, another with eggs, another with bread, another with lard. All the articles are dear, for they have all been brought surreptitiously, and no woman has more to sell than she can hide in her bodice, but the superiority to what the State machine manages to furnish is very striking.

I will put the matter in yet a third form. Three, even so lately as two, years ago, the "N.E.P." still existed; there was free trade, and there was abundance—indeed, the clothes that are worn nowadays, the high boots of men comrades, and the dresses of their womenfolk, were mostly bought in the days of the N.E.P.; it is all being worn to the last thread, and cannot now be replaced.

It is here, in this failure of the socialist system to provide either manufactured goods or even a piece of bread and a pat of butter—butter is one of the rarest commodities in Moscow, and much more difficult to procure than scent—and in the fact that so soon as that system gives way necessities of all kinds are to be procured, that we see not only the bankruptcy of applied socialism, but also the destiny of all Bolshevik five years' plans.

The world, we see, is so made that work only has a value if an individual, be he manager, initiator or contractor, derives profit from it. All the older workmen say: "When I worked for a master, I had everything; now I am myself master I have nothing." I have myself heard those words many times.

Socialist rivalry, the socialist structure, enthusiasm and propaganda, workmen and communist cells, work, work, and, once again, work—the whole atmosphere in which Bolshevia exists and has its being is simply doping. It is obvious that human profit, and especially the profit of that element which directs work, is the natural reward of work. Russia cannot provide this natural reward, and she is merely living on drugs. Hence her work and, still more, the results of that work suggest the output of a drug victim.

In conclusion, I will try to describe the appearance of a Soviet street. All along the line of the houses are endless queues—queues for everything. The rest of the pavement and part of the road is occupied by a tightly-packed crowd, an ant-hill, a conglomeration, a thicket of humanity. In Moscow, pavement and gutter are hidden beneath a crowd infinitely denser than in Paris. But in the middle of the street the proportion is reversed. Even in the busiest streets there is an interval of some two hundred yards between the vehicles. The crowd is untidy and out-at-elbows, dressed like beggars, and the houses it walks under are shabby and filthy. Every now and then there is a foul smell—the sign of a restaurant. When on my return I reached Baranovicze, the first small town in Poland, I had the impression of being in Biarritz. I had always hated the place, but now it seemed to me the height of elegance, and to my eyes the Jews in the streets were dressed like lords.

CHAPTER IV

THE OUTLAW

If I remember rightly, it was at last year's January session of the Council of the League of Nations. The sitting, which took place round a table in a kind of greenhouse by the hotel of the League of Nations, was proceeding on its usual boring, sleepy, monotonous way. Journalists filled all the corridors. Suddenly, as I entered the conference room, I heard shouts rising above a din. What had happened? Somebody was outraging the peculiar dignity characteristic of meetings of the League of Nations, at which it is emphatically not done to betray excitement. One man was waving his arms. I drew the attention of my fellow journalists to what was happening. It turned out that the matter under discussion was the enslavement of niggers which still exists in Liberia.

I remembered this scene of indignation and sympathy in the League of Nations over the existence, south of the equator, of slavery among niggers, when I began my study in Bolshevia of the problem of the "outlaws."

Is an "outlaw" in Bolshevia the same as a

slave? No! But then the "outlaw" is also not a nigger. The "outlaws" in Russia are often people who formerly bought the pictures of foreign masters, who nursed the arts and who were nursed by them, who belonged to the international intellectual coterie of Europe. There is a part of their work, there is a leavening of their thought and emotions, in all the intellectual efforts of Europe. The intellectuals of Europe, at every meeting or congress, should think of them as their colleagues.

The "outlaw" is not the same as a slave—the "outlaw" is almost exactly the same as the mediæval "proscribed" or "banita." He may not be sold or pawned like the slave in Liberia, but, on the other hand, at every step the State deprives him of the possibility of earning, of the possibility of learning, of the possibility of living. I sometimes wondered whether, when next the subject of niggers in Liberia is discussed under the glass roof of the League of Nations at Geneva, I should not find myself shouting out at the top of my voice from the journalists' benches: "What about the outlaws in Russia?"

The "outlaw" has no right to take part in any election—he does not even have a vote in the elections of the village "soviet." The "outlaw" and his children are deprived of the right to attend the higher schools and, should he falsify a document in order to get them into one, he is punished as a criminal. The "outlaw" may not live in the six chief towns of the Union of Soviet Republics; travelling by railway is made exceedingly difficult for him; his children are not received into the primary schools, for these are generally full of the children of the working proletariat; and he may not be a member of any trades union—which means that he cannot obtain any work—which in turn means that he does not receive food cards.

Finally, it is true that it is not permitted to kill an "outlaw" for fun in the streets, but it is possible to summon him before the courts, and as the courts do not judge according to the dry standards of justice, but according to the "dynamics of revolution," practically every court will condemn practically every "outlaw" simply because he is an "outlaw" and is brought before it.

I came across such a case during my journey. The *biednota* (poor community) took his hay from a peasant "outlaw" who owned a horse and two cows. The peasant had nothing left to feed his animals with. The judge, considering the case from the point of view of the "dynamics of revolution," decided that the peasant must give up his animals to his despoilers since, as he now had nothing to feed them with, they were unnecessary for him as they would in any case die of hunger.

I will quote another case from the Soviet publication on "The Legal Forms of Marriage," where this example is given for the orientation of judges as the correct solution. An old, childless peasant couple took as a servant a seventeen-year-old girl, whom they "loved like a daughter." The girl, however, six months later, wanted to marry a man whom the old people did not like. They therefore turned the girl out. The judge ordered the old couple to make over to the girl a part of their land, just as if she had been their daughter, although neither of them had performed any act of adoption. It was sufficient that the judge found that for half a year the old couple had "loved" the girl like a daughter, for the "dynamics of revolution" to produce such an effect on him. I repeat that this is an example, taken from an official publication, explaining to judges what they are to do in difficult cases, and it is given as an example to be followed.

The "outlaw" is beyond the law, he is the object of social revenge.

Someone may ask, How does the "outlaw" live, if he is not a peasant owning a bit of land, since he cannot obtain either work or bread?

How does he live? I have spoken of the

Orthodox priests begging in the cemeteries—who are now even forbidden to do that. The "outlaw" begs, and hides, and changes his name and identification papers; then it is found out that he is an "outlaw"; he is imprisoned, serves his sentence and is released—and again begs and hides. As a matter of fact, this is not a question which will press a Bolshevik against the wall. He will reply calmly that the Union of Soviet Republics does not exist in order to look after the lot of "outlaws." On the contrary, the Union of Socialist Republics exists in order to wipe out the "outlaw."

In particular I was surprised by a conversation I had with the rector of the First Moscow University, M. Kasatkin.

It took place at the beginning of my stay in Russia. On the previous day I had been to the theatre to see a play illustrating the life of the "Red" students. It appeared that an "outlaw," under an assumed name and pretending to be a Bolshevik, had managed to find his way into their company. Which of them was the "outlaw"? The students did not know, but began to organize an investigation. Finally it turned out that the "outlaw" was the most capable student of them all, and the one who had made the greatest progress with his studies. This scene was artistically on a very high plane. Music began to play and on the stage an impressive number of "Red" students began to form a ring in order to enclose the "outlaw" and catch him. The "outlaw" threw himself about like a fish in a net; he ran round the stage like a mouse in a trap, seeking a means of escape; to the shattering sounds of the music the "Red" circle drew in tighter and tighter, until at last they caught him.

Under the influence of this strong, rather sensational scene, all my low, brutal bourgeois instincts broke out. I began to argue with the venerable rector, M. Kasatkin, that it was all so unjust, so unbearable, even from the revolutionary point of view. Shall the son answer for the father's sins? How could they tell that the son of an "outlaw" would not turn out a first-class communist? How could they refuse education because the father is, or was, a rich peasant? I referred to the Great Revolutionary Museum. According to the statistics displayed there it would appear that 73 per cent of the former political criminals would to-day be "outlaws." The revolution in Russia was made by "outlaws." Kropotkin was not only the son of an "outlaw," but was also the son of a prince. Vladimir Ilitch Ulisnov-Lenin himself was a noble—a descendant of nobles with all the paraphernalia of arms and crest.

The rector listened calmly to this ouburst of bourgeois delirium with an ironic but gentle smile. Then he began to explain to me that a social war was being waged—a war of unprecedented strain—a war of life and death with the old social classes. It was no time to trifle with sentiment. They started from the point of view that everybody was influenced by his family, the opinions of his family and generally by his environment. I had spoken of the old revolutionaries; good. But their children might not be revolutionaries—it was quite possible. Even if they broke off altogether from their families, it was not absolutely certain. "If a child has not seen its mother and father since it was three years old, we certainly regard it as a mitigating circumstance, even as a very important mitigating circumstance, but even that does not give us absolute certainty. We consider that the instincts of the former possessing classes are dangerous even when they can only transmit themselves by blood relationship."

In reply to my question as to whether it ever happened that students were turned out, say, in their fourth year at the university because it was discovered that they were children of *kulaks*, M. Kasatkin shrugged his shoulders and said: "Constantly."

M. Kasatkin is not himself an "outlaw." He is by profession a village schoolmaster. Now, as rector of the Moscow University (the richest of all the Russian universities in glory and tradition), he has no trouble with the question of the autonomy of the university, for this does not exist in Bolshevia. M. Kasatkin himself appoints the professors and docents, and, I must confess, I did not gain the impression that he had any doubt as to the adequacy of his knowledge with regard to any of the faculties. He told me, however, that declared communists only filled 5 per cent of the professional chairs in some of the faculties. This percentage, however, is higher in the sciences connected more or less closely with politics, such as sociology, literature, etc.

Now comes the question, who is an "outlaw"?

I took a passionate interest in the "outlaw" question during the first weeks of my stay in Bolshevia. I did not then know that to look for juridical standards in that state is *absolutely* the same as looking for a needle in a haystack.

The constitution of the Soviet Republic, in reply to the question, who is an "outlaw"? says one thing; the election regulations, also published as an official handbook, say another; while in practice I had occasion to confirm still another. In Moscow there are bureaux for the purpose of re-establishing the rights of "outlaws"—these are the bureaux to which the "outlaw" applies in order to get his status back again, to prove that he should not have been made an "outlaw." The "basic outlaws" are: (1) The clergy of all religions; (2) those who were connected in a reactionary sense with political cases during the tsardom; (3) those who exploited hired labour. On this background, as on a canvas, are embroidered every possible combination—often cryingly contradictory one with another. The former *gendarme* is obviously an "outlaw"—unless he is to-day serving in the G.P.U. A qualified engineer who is engaged in a branch of Soviet industry is not an "outlaw," even though he were formerly a manager or a partner of a factory. The peasant who formerly hired a labourer to help him is an "outlaw." Every former landowner should be and is an "outlaw," but this does not prevent, in one case a Polish count, formerly the owner of huge estates, in another, a Polish baron, from being eminent Bolsheviks. I do not mention this in order to suggest that the opinion of the Bolshevik commissar decides who is and who is not an "outlaw." It is not anybody's opinion which decides, but the pitch and direction of Bolshevik agitation at a given moment. The man who, two years ago, was glaringly an "outlaw," to-day may be recognized as not being one, if his case is reopened—and *vice versa*. As I write this, there is a fierce war on priests, mullahs and *kulaks*. Therefore every peasant who does not join a *kolchoz*, and who can be attacked on any slight grounds, will be made an "outlaw." The most poverty-stricken peasant may be declared an "outlaw"—if in his particular village there doesn't happen to be a peasant who is better off.

The institution of "outlaws" has therefore a double character—offensive and defensive. It has a defensive character in so far as it is aimed at clearing off the face of the earth, or at least crushing down, economically suffocating, the class of society suspected of harbouring an unfavourable attitude towards the Soviet *régime*. This is the strangling of the class which *might* possibly form the basis of a counter-revolution. It has an offensive character in so far as it approximates to the paper target used for firing practice. Day in, day out, in Bolshevia there is the need for excitement, for political hashish. The "outlaws" are the institution on which the revolutionary temperaments unload themselves.

The same—and in even a greater degree—can be said of the *vreditels* (enemies). The *vreditel* is a man charged with sabotage of Soviet labour.

The world has heard of the elaborate proceedings against certain *vreditels*, the Shakhtinski case, the Ramzin case, etc. According to everything I was able to hear, the Bolsheviks exaggerate the prevalence of the *vreditel* to an extraordinary extent. The *vreditel*, while in prison, signs a confession attributing to him crimes which he did not commit—and in this manner avoids the punishment of death without trial. If Russia were a country which was bursting with political protestations, with terrorist activity, where political organizations were working everywhere underground, I would willingly believe in the existence of "vreditelism" on a big scale. But in Russia we have an entirely different state of affairs. Counter-revolutionary activity is hardly discernible. There is a great dislike of the Government—70 or 80 per cent of the whole population hate the Soviets with an explicit, open, desperate, bitter hatred; but it is a hatred which cannot transform itself into any planned action—an impotent hatred. I regard the socialist economic system as idiocy. I have already described how it appears in practice. But the Bolsheviks cannot confess to the masses that hunger, poverty, lack of everything, and various incidental catastrophes, happen because their economic system is idiotic. Some explanation has to be found to explain the deficiencies of the system and the disasters that befall, and the simplest and easiest, the most convincing explanation is the *vreditel*—that there are people, hating the Soviets, who are deliberately working against them.

The masses believe this. I saw a film on this subject—"The Pointsman was Guilty." This represented a railway accident, for which, according to the administration of the railway, the pointsman was responsible, while the real perpetrator of the crime is the station-master, a former civil servant, who, when he says "Leningrad," in his thoughts corrects it to "Petrograd," and then to "St. Petersburg," and sees a vision of himself in the Tsar's uniform, sees the streets thronged with smart people and girls. In this manner Bolshevik agitation provides an explanation of why the economic system suffers crash after crash, and intensifies the suspiciousness of the masses. Robespierre said "suspiciousness in politics is the same as jealousy in love—you can never have too much of it." Russia for ten years has been living and dying in a bloody, suspicious, evil ecstasy comparable to that of the revolutionary year 1793, that "terrible year."

CHAPTER V

AN ANSWER TO THE SECOND QUESTION

ONLY now, after having sketched in the background of life in Russia, can I permit myself to ask whether the reader has understood my reply to the second question which I asked myself when leaving for Bolshevik Russia. It will be recalled that this question was as follows: "Whether in the fight between Bolshevik Russian centralization and the nationalistic forces of decentralization, the former will win or the latter." I repeat the question in the form in which I put it to myself before my departure for Russia. This question, however, is in its very essence falsely put.

In the first place, in Bolshevik Russia there is no Bolshevik *Russian* centralization, but only Bolshevik centralization. The expression, "scratch a Bolshevik and you will find a Russian chauvinist," no longer contains any truth.

In the second place, the real struggle in the provinces is against the efforts of Bolshevik headquarters to impose on the provinces separate languages, which are objected to by the inhabitants. The fight of these inhabitants (in Kieff,

Kharhov, Minsk, etc.) against enforced ukrianization and white russification is of infinitely more importance than the tiny and feeble signs of a nationalistic movement in these provinces, which signs never assume the character of a mass movement.

In the third place, the Bolsheviks are more or less right when they assert that they do not persecute Ukrainian or White Russian nationalists (these last must be sought for with a microscope!), but persecute counter-revolution. This is true, with certain reservations. In Bolshevik Russia national feeling as such is forbidden in general; the possession or demonstration of national feeling is therefore by its very nature anti-Bolshevik. The Bolsheviks therefore are not correct when they say that they do not persecute nationalism, but they are right when they assert that they persecute Ukrainian nationalism as an anti-Bolshevik phenomenon. In any case, it is Russian patriotism, Great Russian patriotism, which is particularly picked out for persecution, and is crushed wherever it is found.

All national feelings are persecuted, all patriotism is crushed, but no language. Everyone must go to a school where his native language is spoken, with the exception of the Russian. If I live in Kieff, and am a Ukrainian, a Pole or a German,

I am provided with a school for my child where the teaching is in its native language. If I am a Russian living in Kieff, great pressure is brought on me to send my child to a Ukrainian school.

The same state of affairs obtains in each of the national republics, not only those belonging to the Union, but the dominion republics and even dominion districts (*oblasti*). At the beginning of the present school year (1931–32) the university in Kazan was to be tatarized. The greater part of the schools are already tatarized, and this year the process is being applied to still larger numbers. I travelled with a teacher of one of these schools. He was in despair. He had to learn the Tatar language, although he did not know a word of it, despite the fact that he had for twenty years lived in Kazan. It must also be realized that all the nationalities, beginning with the Tatars, have received new alphabets. The Tatars and certain other nationalities had their own alphabets, but the greater part of the tribes—some of which number only several scores of thousands—had no alphabet. For all of them alphabets have been constructed, but they are Latin alphabets. In this connection, I put the following question to a Bolshevik who occupies a responsible position in the organization dealing with questions of nationality:

"The Bolsheviks do not encourage a separatist feeling of nationality—on the contrary, they rather discourage it in accordance with the slogan of internationalism. The system of giving a child instruction in its own language is based, not on a recognition of the necessity of cultivating his separate nationality, but on the desire to make it generally possible for an uneducated person to obtain instruction, in accordance with the dictum of Lenin—'It is easier for everyone to read in his own language than in a foreign language.' Taking this into consideration, I do not understand why you have hit particularly on the Latin alphabet. Your man from the steppes of Asia or in the Far North is a Soviet citizen. The centre of the Soviets is located in Moscow; it might be expected, therefore, that in the course of his life he would constantly meet with the Russian language—in other words, he will be obliged to learn the Russian alphabet, and must consequently learn two alphabets instead of one. This presumably will be a burden for him and will handicap his learning. Why, therefore, when introducing alphabets for these tribes, do you not give them a Russian alphabet?"

In reply to this, I listened to the following:—

"I will reply to your question with another question. Do you think that we shall for long continue to use our Russian alphabet? You have probably yourself heard the latinization of the Russian alphabet spoken of, and there is no doubt that this will take place in a short time."

Kieff is a thoroughly Russian city. For two days I walked about its streets keeping my ears open, but not once did I hear the Ukrainian language spoken. I went to two Ukrainian theatres, but it never occurred to anybody to speak to me other than in Russian. It was not difficult, it is true, to get together several literary people who spoke the Ukrainian language to meet me. But I have the feeling that it is with regard to Ukrainians in Kieff the same as with regard to Lithuanians in Wilno—if one specially wants to, one can always get several together in one room, but to hear the Ukrainian language in the streets of Kieff is almost as difficult as it is to hear Lithuanian in Wilno. On the other hand, all the public offices use the Ukrainian language. The explanations in museums and former churches are chiefly given in the Ukrainian language; and finally, all the signboards in the streets are Ukrainian. For example, a kiosk with Russian newspapers (there will be several Ukrainian newspapers lying on one side) has its signboard printed only in Ukrainian. The Polish language is heard much more in the streets of Kieff than the Ukrainian.

There is, moreover, an Institute of Polish Culture, something in the way of a Polish Academy, a Polish Pedagogic Seminary, two colossal Polish schools, a Polish section in the Faculty of Medicine, and a Polish section in the Dramatic Institute. The maps showing the distribution of nationalities which are hung up in the ethnographic museums are thickly painted with the colour indicating the entirely Polish communities which inhabit a considerable part of the Ukrainian countryside. In Kieff the Polish theatre possesses a troupe of seventy actors and an auditorium greater than that of the official Ukrainian theatre.

(How delightful Kieff is—one of the most beautiful cities in the world! When I was there, the Dnieper had overflowed its banks. There was a lovely view of the city—that "prince in a cloak of gold and green"—from the hills on which stands the inspired Saint Vladimir—under whose arm the Bolsheviks have thrust a wireless loud-speaker. The whole of Kieff breathed the air of the Dnieper and smelt of may. Everything was saturated with the perfume of the may trees. . . .)

Among the Bolsheviks themselves voices are raised in protest against the forced Ukrainization of the Russian population living in the Ukraine. There are "comrades" who declare: "It's all very well the peasant being Ukrainian, but it must not be forgotten that besides the peasant there is the proletariat, the Russian proletariat, for whom it is difficult to acquire a language it has never spoken. By all means take into consideration the needs of the peasant, but also those of the proletariat in the schools and in the Government offices; and don't force Ukrainization in those directions where it is not necessary, and where there is no Ukrainian population." Thus the representatives of the "left wing"; thus the Trotsky Jews. The Jews are defenders of the Russian language against the crazy nationality policy of the Union.

This kind of declaration and argument is fought against as being Trotsky-ism. In general, over the whole territory of the Union, in the *profsojuz* (trades unions) and everywhere else, the Bolshevik governing circles show the greatest zeal, not in fighting unsatisfied nationalistic pretensions, as is generally supposed, but in fighting the revolt of the impatient Russian population who in Kubania are required to speak Ukrainian, in Kazan Tatar, in Minsk Litewsk, Orsza, Mogilev, Vitebsk, Polotsk—White Russian.

I went to Bolshevia with a ready-made theory, for which I only wanted to find support and arguments on the spot. I felt sure that just as Pilsudski and Slavek, in their fight with tsardom, had used socialism as a hammer, as a tool for forcing Polish independence into existence, so *anti-Bolshevism* would be used by *nationalistic* forces for breaking up Russia. I remember that as I stood on the steps of the train when leaving for Russia, I declared that the strategic key of the future of Russia was the Ukraine; if the Ukraine achieved independence, Russia would fall to pieces; if the Bolsheviks succeeded in holding her in their grip, they would easily manage the other nationalities. This method of reasoning cannot be called illogical, and yet how false, how contrary to reality it is! It is not the case that anti-Bolshevism is the tool of the national movements, but that the national movements are a parasite on anti-Bolshevism. The majority of the inhabitants of the Russian Empire do not want Bolshevism; the point is, they do not know what they do want. A negative policy—no matter to what point it is developed—does not correspond in the slightest degree with any constructive idea. The nationalistic movement in the Ukraine finds a response because it is anti-Bolshevik. Thus sympathy was awakened by the case against Jefremov and his companions who, as a matter of fact, were probably falsely accused of hob-nobbing with the German Consul, and quite certainly falsely accused of contact with Poland,

and who, in their ceremonial "acts of repentance," confessed to these sins which they did not commit. But this does not mean that every serious anti-Bolshevik movement on a broad Russian scale—in other words, an imperial movement—does not awake ten times as much sympathy, a hundred times as much hope, in Kieff, Kharkov, Odessa, or Minsk as elsewhere.

There remains only one question. How is it that such a nation as the Great Russian, who undoubtedly dominate the whole Russian Empire, not only by force of tradition and as the successors of the tsars, but also as the real governing power, exert their power in the direction of paring off their own dominions, even of reducing artificially the area in which their language is spoken, in order to ensure the domination of certain nationalities and tribes in certain areas?

This phenomenon can be explained in two ways: mystically and realistically.

Mystically, it can be explained by saying that it is only another form of the imperialism of the Great Russian people. By protecting nationalism—but incidentally taking from it the essential substance of every form of nationalism—it connects all these nationalities and tribes into a solid ring round Moscow, thus ensuring the latter a predominating rôle.

This, however, is too mystical, too paradoxical an explanation. The realistic explanation is quite different. Patriotism is an idea which is contradictory to Bolshevism. Patriotism is not only an idea, it is a force. I will not try to explain the extraordinary things which happen in Russia by pointing out that the dictator of Russia is a Georgian, and that there are so many foreigners and Jews in the Government of that unhappy country. I will avoid explanations which all too many people find convincing. I prefer to think that the Bolsheviks, considering that patriotism is an idea and a force most inimical to them, fear above all Great Russian patriotism, as the Great Russian nation is not only the most numerous, but the most capable, the most talented and the strongest.

The idea propagated at one time by the "change of era" party that, while of course Bolshevia is Bolshevia, there is yet Russia in that Bolshevia, and that working for Bolshevia is in effect working for Russia, was at one time tolerated and even favourably regarded by communists; but now that idea is considered dangerous, and as calling for suppression at all costs. After religion and the *kulaks*, the idea of Russian patriotism comes in for the greatest measure of persecution—and the Bolsheviks are not particular about the means they use. Nevertheless, the last stage of this fight has not yet been reached.

What I shall have to say later on about Asia in Bolshevia will supplement the above remarks. I understand perfectly well that in writing what I have I am radically opposing those convictions which it is pleasant for us to hold, and which—like everything banal—have an easy task in defending their right of existence.

CHAPTER VI

LAUDETUR JEZUS CHRISTUS

In the Nansen school in Moscow I had a talk with two seventh-form students who represented the autonomous body of the students in the school. "What would you do if one of your fellow-students robbed a member of the class?" I asked of them.

One of the bright young Bolsheviks split up the case logically into six possibilities. He explained the procedure to me: how the case would be considered by the class committee, then by the school committee, and how the decision must finally be approved by the school management. He foresaw all the mitigating circumstances which might affect the student guilty of the theft, and generally adopted rather a humane and merciful attitude.

"And what would you do if it were found out that one of your fellow-students had been to service in church and had sung together with the choir?"

The boy answered categorically: "There is no place for such a one amongst us."

The procedure for turning out such a boy was

much simpler. The case would go at once to the school committee. On my insisting that there might in the case of this infringement also be mitigating circumstances, the boy agreed that this might be the case if it were done in circumstances arising out of dire need in order to earn money. "But if it should be shown that he deceived us all the time, that he pretended that he shared our opinion, but was in fact religious, then, of course, he would be expelled."

Service in a church is extraordinarily moving. There is the feeling that each person who attends the service is performing an act of courage, is endangering himself and his. There goes an old, very old man with a stick, in a fur coat with what was once a luxurious beaver collar. To-day the fur is ragged, the old man's cheeks tremble. And there go women, carrying the Bolshevik newspaper *Pravda*. They unfold their *Pravda* and take out a prayer-book, an old-fashioned prayer-book dating from the nineteenth century. He who would go through a really moving and exalting experience should visit Moscow and attend mass—a ceremony much more exalting and moving than the most wonderful service in the basilica of St. Peter's at Rome. Those who come here risk all. Beyond the walls of the church reign force, terror, the whole strength of a huge empire turned in hate against the prayers whispered in that church. Those prayers seem holier there than anywhere else, and every sacrament performed in that atmosphere of poverty, fear and threat seems different; it would be terrible to think of the breaking of marriage or other vows made within those holy, trebly holy, poor walls.

In Leningrad there are eight Roman Catholic churches functioning, but there are only three Roman Catholic priests. Each Catholic church is the private property of the State. It may be leased only to twenty persons, who sign an undertaking that they are responsible for the building. It follows from this that amongst the Polish population of Leningrad there are 160 heroes. One of the repressive measures employed is the constant demand for the repair and restoration of the church. The church of St. Catherine in Leningrad is constantly undergoing forced renovation.

Although it insists on these repairs and renovations, the Soviet Government does not provide any materials. In spite of the extraordinary lack of fuel in Leningrad in winter, the churches are required to be heated. At the same time, on the maps of Leningrad which are still hanging, from N.E.P. times, in the Leningrad clubs, the bars and the Russian and Roman

Catholic churches are painted black, indicating that they are factors of decomposition, while the clubs, schools and "houses of culture" are painted red—the colour of the future.

There is a terrible shortage of priests in Bolshevia. New priests may not be ordained; the teaching of theology is forbidden. Particularly in White Russia is there a dearth of clergy. There were serious cases there of recantation, but in comparison—but no, we will make no comparisons. I will explain later why we will make no comparisons. If there have been a few sad cases there of defeat in the terrible battle with this terribly superior power, how many cases have there been of heroism! Bishop Malecki—what a hero! He will surely be canonized. The aged man, on being released from the prison in which he was incarcerated with the late Archbishop Cieplak, and with the murdered priest Budkievicz, could have come to Poland together with the Archbishop. He refused to come. He who was formerly a Polish patriot now declared that he was a Soviet citizen, and he remained behind with those unhappy inhabitants of Leningrad. Further, with pride, with a greatness of heart, such as can be met with nowhere but in that land of terror, he remained as a loyal Soviet subject. He did not interfere in politics—that, he said, was not the business of a priest. His great work, his holy mission, was to bring the solace of religion to those thirsting for it, to drive away despair from those who were weak in spirit, to administer the grace of the Catholic faith. A few months ago the Bolsheviks arrested Bishop Malecki—and took him no one knows where. No one was able to suggest to me any way in which he was in fault towards the Soviet authorities. On the contrary, all confirmed that his activities were characterized by great punctiliousness towards the Soviet authorities. The Bolsheviks arrested him for no offence and without giving any pretext—which is not their usual practice. It is not known whether he is alive. Meanwhile, the League of Nations looks after the niggers in Liberia.

I said, "we will not make any comparisons." We do not need to compare, for every Orthodox person, every Bolshevik, and everybody else in Russia will confirm that the Roman Catholic Church as far as concerns the cohesion of its priests and its followers, is beyond any comparison with other religions. But in order to explain why I do not wish to make comparisons, I must do something that is not generally done—I must make a sort of confession of something I did and which afterwards filled me with disgust for my behaviour. I met once an Orthodox priest, begging for alms. Giving him a few worthless Soviet roubles—the official value of which is two roubles to the dollar, but which I bought in Warsaw at Zł 3.65 (about two shillings) for ten—I said to him in Polish "*prosze*" ("please"—"here you are"). The priest raised his eyes and looked at me.

I understood that this is not the time to remember in any shape or form the wrongs inflicted on us by the Orthodox Church. The tragedy is too great, the suffering too severe, the humiliation too terrible.

Out of the three hundred odd Orthodox churches in Moscow, only thirty or forty are functioning, and those the smallest and poorest. The Church has been split up into several independent organizations. But the favouring of some of these organizations has ceased. To-day the persecution of all of them has brought together the priests of the new, reformed Bolshevik Church with those of the old Church of Tikhon. Sects were formerly tolerated; now the organizing of a sect is punishable by shooting. In one of the anti-religious museums I saw shirts sewn all over with awkward-looking crosses. This was the sect of "crusaders"—bearers of the cross, who sewed crosses all over their linen. The owners of these shirts—so ran the inscription—had been shot. Formerly the socialists rather sympathized with the sectarians, who objected to conscription to the army. The Government of the Tsar (in those bad old times) had a lot of trouble with those sects. The Bolsheviks shoot every sectarian who, in the name of Christian pacifism, refuses to join the army. They shoot them by the hundred.

In order to shoot an Orthodox priest it is sufficient to find in his lodging a piece of money with the Tsar's imprint, or to find in his attic an old forgotten flag with the national Russian colours, or an ikon with an inscription mentioning the Tsar. Any of these objects may by accident happen to be in any lodging. But all that is nothing in comparison with the fiendish torture inflicted on all religious feeling. Articles which are the objects of the greatest cult, holy articles connected with the deepest mystery of religion, are exhibited deliberately in the most shameful manner. A miraculous ikon is shown surrounded with shameless pictures depicting drunken priests; the relics of the saints of the Orthodox Church are exhibited with a bottle of vodka under the arm.

Before going to Russia, having heard of these anti-religious museums, I had formed the opinion that they were centres of peaceful persuasion, that religion was shown in the light of its historical developments with a view to arousing doubts as to whether our present-day religion is the same as it was in the beginning. But nothing of the sort. The religious museums are not designed for persuasion, but with the object of holding up religion to a blasphemous, wicked, mad scorn, with the object of torturing religious feeling in the most brutal and shameless manner.

Let us look at the principles of Bolshevik atheism.

Its first characteristic is that Bolshevism does not limit itself to the refusal to recognize the divinity of Jesus Christ, but generally denies that Christ ever existed as an historical figure, as the founder of a religion in Palestine. "History proves that such a person as Jesus Christ never existed."

It is shown that the Christian religion always went hand in hand with the rich classes, that it aroused militarism; that the Archangel Michael was a knight, etc. Whole rows and columns of sneers on this subject. And when the Bolsheviks come to the Crucifix, to the martyrdom of Jesus Christ, they argue that in this manner the bourgeoisie persuaded the masses that their duty was to suffer with resignation. "Your God suffered passively, and you must suffer passively, and bear with all kinds of persecution."

Finally, there is the motto which, printed in

red, hangs in nearly every Orthodox church: "Christianity was always the religion of the exploiting classes." How ridiculous that is!

Bruno Jasinski, author of that amusing book *I Burn Paris*, expresses his enthusiasm for the world of antique culture and his hatred of the Christians. But who first said, "Love thy neighbour as thyself"? Who first gave the order to love the poor, to respect poverty? The Bolsheviks themselves base their degenerate, terrorist policy on the exaltation of the proletariat, the poverty-stricken; but the conception was not theirs.

The pagans thought otherwise. Petronius says to Vinicius, "Shall I then love the slaves who bear my chair, the Egyptians who heat the fires in my baths? By the white knees of the Graces, I swear to thee that though I would I could not. In Rome there are at least a hundred thousand people with crooked arms, or enlarged knees, or wasted calves, or round eyes, or too large heads. Dost tell me to love them too? He who loves beauty cannot, for that very reason, love ugliness."

It is to be noted that where the Christian says "love" the Bolshevik puts "hate"; where the Christian says "mercy" the Bolshevik again says "hate." Where Christianity gave peace, love and happiness, there Bolshevism has given materialism, terror, degeneration.

The Bolsheviks are people who hate Christ. That is their greatest hatred. They know that they lie, but they lie with outrageous persistence.

"Christianity is a religion of the exploiting classes!"

I had a long talk with an intelligent Bolshevik leader. I asked him how they could so calumniate a religion which teaches love for one's neighbour. He replied: "We forgive only dead gods. Christ is a living God."

Yes, Christ is a living God.

In Bolshevia it is forbidden to ring the church bells. The Orthodox priest has no right to live; nothing is permitted him; he has no bread card, he is an outcast. The child who prays is expelled from school. The man who prays loses his job. At every step religious feeling is insulted in the most savage manner. The churches are pulled down. Every religious picture is defaced. The monks are in prison, or have been shot in hundreds. And after all that, the foreigner is told: "We do not persecute religion!"

Let those of us who have got out of the habit of praying, who have forgotten their "Our Father," go to Russia. There their lips will automatically form themselves into a prayer.

CHAPTER VII

WOMAN, UNVEIL THYSELF

The matters which I touch on here should really be discussed in an international forum. The views should be heard not only of those who know Bolshevia, but also of those who know Asia. There is no doubt that this is a matter of the greatest concern, not only in regard to the future of Bolshevism, but also from the point of view of the future of the whole cultured world. The point at issue is: Where is Bolshevism more dangerous—in Asia or in Europe?

If I were an English journalist, I should certainly have far more to say about Russia than I am able to. But, judging from what I have observed myself, I am prepared to support the view that Bolshevism is more dangerous in Asia. We in Poland are the direct neighbours of Bolshevia, but nevertheless Bolshevism is a greater danger for those countries possessing territory in Asia.

The third question which I went to Russia to answer was: "What is the nature and extent of the influence of Asia on Bolshevik Russia?"

Even after entering Bolshevik Russia, my

attitude towards this question went through several evolutions. At first I recognized that the question was quite silly, and that Asia exerted no influence at all—other than the fashion of wearing *tubeteyeks* on the head. Later I veered round to my original intuition. Now I would formulate my answer to the question in the following manner.

We cannot speak of the influence on Moscow of the culture or of the national spirit of the Asiatic peoples, for Bolshevism destroys differences in culture and all signs of spiritual culture. Nevertheless, the influence of Asia on Bolshevia may be symbolized by saying that Stalin is very much more an Asiatic than Lenin was, or could be, or wanted to be.

During the whole of the nineteenth century the Russian intelligentsia was divided into westerners (*zapadniki*) and slavophiles. The present Euro-asiatics are the worthy heirs of the slavophiles. Contact with Europe and the separateness of Russia were opposite theses. What is Bolshevism —westernism or slavophilism?

I might reply here that the whole question is too literary, too bourgeois and counter-revolutionary, to be worth consideration. But let us contemplate for a moment a literary analogy. Dostoyevski, that writer of genius, convict, prophet and propagandist of Russian monarchy (the spiritual father of the "black hundreds," as Stanislas Brzozovski, I think for the first time, called him), presents to us in *The Karamazov Brothers* a portrait of the old Karamazov—a Russian noble, a drunkard and a scoundrel. In the company of other drunkards, Karamazov walks through the streets and meets a hump-backed beggar woman shuffling along in the gutter—a crippled monster, a hysterical degenerate. The drunken men began to discuss whether it is possible to have love relations with such a creature. Old Karamazov is ready to take up the challenge. The result of the relationship between this degenerate noble and this wretched hump-back is the birth of Smerdiakov—he is Karamazov's son, his lackey and his murderer.

Bolshevism is without doubt westernism. Its father was Marx, and the German books read by the Russian students in blue uniforms with buttons bearing double-headed eagles. But Bolshevism is first of all Smerdiakov, the creature born of the relations of a drunken intellect with the hysteria of beastliness. Bolshevism is urbanization. The ideal of the Bolshevik paradise of the future is factories, machines, forests of chimneys. As Mahomet promised houris, so Bolshevism promises you a powerful machine over your head and a loud-speaker by your ear at all hours of the day and night. The conviction that the town is worth more than the countryside finds its expression in the constitution of the Union of Soviet Republics, clearly and symbolically. One delegate to the central representative body falls to every 25,000 citizens of towns and to every 125,000 inhabitants of the countryside. So that a country workman is worth only a fifth of a town workman. The same principle applies to the favouring of town workmen for appointments in the civil service or places in the universities.

Asia cannot be urbanized, but it can be revolutionized. I have already written that I do not believe in the industrialization of Russia. I have seen enormous, gigantic, magnificent factories. I wondered at the huge scale on which they were built, at the American *tempo*. But at the end there is always something that does not fit in, and the whole structure does not fulfil its function. I do not believe that the industry of other countries can be overtaken by people whose government has brought about such a state of things that in that enormous agricultural country it is impossible to find a spare piece of bread, and who have pushed poverty and lack of everything to a degree not recorded for centuries and unknown during the greatest famines, catastrophes and wars. I do not believe that the socialist system can pass through this successfully, when on every hand I observe the absolute victory over this system of the hole-and-corner dealers, threatened as they are at every step with death. How magnificently symbolic it is that the Soviet State imprisons speculators who, having paid the peasants more for their grain than the State, have succeeded in carrying it to the starving provinces. The "speculator" paid the producer more, smuggled it away, and still was able to supply the hungry provinces and rescue the starving. And, as a reward, he was put in prison. I confess that the fact that he sits in prison is not for me a convincing argument for prophesying that the economic system of the Soviets will emerge victorious.

For particulars of "speculators" of this type I have gone to a book called *Grabbers and Swindlers —Practices of Speculative Capital*, published by the Commissariat of Justice of the Ukrainian Socialist Soviet Republic.

Although I do not believe that the principles of economics will bow the knee to and follow the dictates of an angry revolution, I fear the revolutionization of Asia. Let us take Northern Asia, let us take the example of that Academy for the Peoples of the North, which I described earlier. Did the Tsar's Government ever think of creating for itself such propagandists amongst the tent-dwellers?

Kolchozes for catching fish operate in the icy waters along the northern coast of Asia. I saw detailed reports of these *Kolchozes*. When a western Russian, a qualified mechanic, for example, accepts Bolshevism, he goes through a severe "breaking in." He must leave his religion, the religion which he knew and had absorbed in its philosophical form, subtle, noble and poetic. He must part with a sufficiency of food, with his bottle of wine or beer, and with the freedom and liberalism of his thoughts and convictions; with his canary in its cage, and his tablecloth on the table—with his football. Now he will be hungry and ragged, and will even stand in a queue to get a Soviet newspaper. But what sort of "breaking in" must the inhabitant of the Arctic Circle go through, this member of the fishing *Kolchoz* in the Arctic Ocean? His religion, his gods? He has forgotten them before he has learned the first rules of arithmetic. The elementary school has wiped out entirely his primitive ideas of religion, and what the Bolsheviks give him—those few crumbs of civilization—is sufficient to make him a disciple of this bread-giver. The strength of Bolshevism lies in its recognizing him as a brother. The Asiatic peoples have been persecuted; the Bolsheviks treat them as they treated that workman I described, who took a course in history and became the director of a museum. The Bolsheviks take a Khirghiz or Kalmuck and make him a minister of state; they force up representatives of the Asiatic nationalities into the highest posts in the State; they give those nationalities alphabets, schools and universities. It is true they are only bluffing when they promise to give them agricultural machinery. But everyone will understand that when such a *Kolchoz* as I have spoken of is being organized, the most intelligent of the natives, the most energetic and worthy of them, are easily persuaded to join it, and begin to work with it. In other words, Bolshevism is based on a selection of the people, and carries out that selection itself. Just as in Russia the *kulak*, the intelligent peasant, is against Bolshevism, so amongst these wild brutes the best elements are in favour of Bolshevism.

On the other hand, true to their ideology of supporting the lowest, the Bolsheviks, when they find in one district one tribe dominating and another held in subjection by the first, protect the second and push it forward by all sorts of artificial means. But this selection of the weakest —like the election of the best elements described above—results in the creation of spheres of influence in Asiatic territory strongly supporting the Soviets.

In reply to my question, What is most threatening for communism in Asia—the capitalist countries, or the growth of Asiatic nationalism? I received from a highly-placed Bolshevik the categorical answer: that only and exclusively the capitalist countries count, viz., England, France, Japan and America. I don't know how this answer should be understood. But let us consider the factor which might have threatened most the expansion of the Soviets, and observe it from a distance.

I am referring to Islam. In 1927 I wrote some studies about contemporary Turkey. I have no sympathy with Kemal Pasha. He has brought about the realization of a nationalism more extreme than was conceived of by Wilson. I call "nationalism" the doctrine that it is sufficient to have a separate language and ethnical community to form a separate state. Nationalist Turkey expels from its borders the minorities, such as the Greeks, and, in defiance of history, embodies the ideal of the "national state" in all its senseless extravagance. Old Turkey, with its Caliph, who was a power in the whole Mussulman world, was a typical example of the imperialistic State; the present Turkey is a record example of what nationalist excesses can bring a country to.

Nationalism in Turkey is anti-historical, absolutely democratic, anti-religious. Islam is persecuted in Turkey as orthodoxy is in Russia. While Turkey was formerly a powerful source for the aspirations of Islam, now it is Turkey that drives a knife into the back of an Islam which is in the throes of a struggle with Bolshevism. There is a big difference between the Young Turks and the Kemalists. The Young Turks were reformers, something in the style of the Polish "patriots" of the 3rd of May epoch; but the Young Turks did not wish to give up anything of their imperialist, historic traditions of a great State. Enver Bey fell in the fight with Bolshevism in Central Asia in 1922. Kemal Pasha, for the sake of the independence of the purely Turkish part, gave up everything else. The existence of Kemal is a factor facilitating to an enormous extent the expansion of communism in Asia.

Islam could have been such a barrier against Bolshevik expansion as cannot easily be found anywhere else in Asia. Evidence that this view is held by the Bolsheviks themselves can be found in the fact that, whereas Bolshevism has dealt with Christian orthodoxy in an utterly merciless and ruthless fashion, it has not gone to such lengths with Islam. In several countries in the Caucasus and in Central Asia the Soviets recognized marriage celebrated according to the Shariate, and in Dagestan for a certain period the Shariate form of marriage was even obligatory, and even communists had to conform to it. This is no longer the case, but Islam continues to play an infinitely greater rôle in the habits and life of the people than Christian orthodoxy is permitted to play.

But what is there behind Islam? Kemal, who persecutes and destroys it; Amannulah, who wanted to be another Peter the Great, but who finished, not with a St. Petersburg, but with a big scandal; the Shah Riza, who must first of all fight the narrow reactionism of his own clergy! Retrogression, the blind, reactionary, stupid priesthoods of Islam and other Asiatic religions; that is one side of the medal. The other is the fact that the nationalisms which are being born and are to become the vital forces in Asia are only nationalisms, devoid of higher ideals, just such as Kemalism. Perhaps the Bolsheviks are right, therefore, when they say that they only have to reckon in Asia with the capitalistic States.

We have mentioned the retrogression in Persia and in Afghanistan. The Islamic reactionaries fought against the emancipation of women, just as our Conservatives did, until they were convinced that as soon as a woman gets a vote she votes for the priest, for Hindenburg, and for Mr. Baldwin. The Soviets, on the other hand, exert all their influence to effect the emancipation of the Mussulman women. They have achieved results in this direction which are quite imposing. In Usbekestan 60 per cent of the chairmen of the rural Soviets are women. I shall suggest later on that woman is only a temporary "hanger-on" of the Soviets. But for the time being it can be said of the Soviets concerning woman that "they rise by her," rather than that "they perish by her." They doff her *tchadra*, her veil, and they find in her a powerful ally.

Finally, then, I reply to the question regarding the influence of Asia on Bolshevia, that Asiatic problems play a much greater rôle in the U.S.S.R. than in the Russia of the Tsar. I was always of the opinion that of the three ways to political expansion which Russia could choose, viz., in the West, Poland (Catherine II), the Balkans (Alexander II and Sazonov), the Asiatic East (Witte and particularly Wilhelm II as adviser to Nicholas II), the right way was the last. That is the way the Soviets have chosen—for the time being. Formerly, the State official, the minister of the Tsar, often visited Nice; the Soviet high official more often travels to Tashkent, Samarkand, and Chita.

CHAPTER VIII

YOUTH IN BOLSHEVIA

From what I have already written the reader will be able to imagine the reply to my third question: What does Russian youth look like, this youth brought up in the belief that religious feeling is a kind of sexual hysteria? The young Bolshevik gets very little real learning. Education, as we generally conceive it, aims at giving the pupil a foundation of knowledge and training his mind to work logically; in Bolshevia education has nothing in common with this. To learn in Bolshevia means to learn to explain everything, from archæological discoveries to the pictures of Picasso, by the class-war and by its relation to production. It resembles not so much education as scholasticism, theological dialectics, such as were taught in the monastic schools in the Middle Ages. Amusing examples of scholastic problems, such as "how many angels can you get on to the head of a pin?" come to mind when contemplating the Bolshevik system. The rôle played in the courts by the "dynamics of revolution," which require of the judge that he shall not be concerned to deal out justice, but only to *intensify the revolution*, is paralleled in the Russian schools and universities, where teaching has to submit to the requirements of "revolution dialectics"—that is, a bending of all scientific observation to make it fit the theories of Marx and the compilations of Lenin.

The result of this brand of teaching is, at least from our point of view, pitiable. The children in the schools know very little; but the Bolsheviks may be satisfied, for the children who leave Bolshevik schools are incapable of understanding anything except in terms of the class-war. I emphasize the words "are incapable," and would like the reader to realize that the children really *are incapable*. They are incapable of understanding Shakespeare except in relation to Marx, they are incapable of understanding Christianity otherwise than as a huckster's trick for throwing dust in the eyes of the working classes; they are incapable of thinking as we think, freely, independently, without forcing our brains into an iron helmet.

The child is from its earliest years caught into the maelstrom of Bolshevik ideas. These are some of the titles of the games in a toyshop for children: *polit-lotto*, "Catch up and overtake," "Scythe and hammer," *kolchoz*, "Aviation battle," etc.

The influence of the family on the child is limited because the family has little to do with it. The child must spend its time in school, or before that, in the crêche. It eats there. Nevertheless, the capacity of the schools is not sufficient to meet the requirements of the juvenile population, in spite of Soviet statistics. In Moscow itself lots of children are compelled to hang about owing to lack of room in the schools. As far as the crêches are concerned, I must describe my own observation. I visited the magnificent "house of culture" for Leningrad workmen near the Narvska Gate. The house was built by the Bolsheviks, and is imposing in its size; there are five auditoria, each of which is capable of holding two thousand people. The house is built for twenty thousand workmen. "Every woman," explained my guide, "who comes here may, while she is resting, leave her child in the special crêche provided." I saw what that "every woman" meant when I was shown the crêche. It consisted of two rooms, each of which could hold from fifteen to twenty children. There were several cradles, two or three small tables, and a few little chairs. Surprised, I asked where the other rooms were. I learned that this was the whole crêche. This is very characteristic of the way things are done in Soviet Russia. A thing is made with an imposing exterior, but inside it doesn't "hang together!"

In the schools the children are constantly

required to fill up questionnaires. By this means the small child is made to serve the purposes of the spy system. The child must fill in these huge questionnaires, containing many questions relating to the manner of living of its parents. These questionnaires are material for the G.P.U. The child never realizes how often it is an informer against its parents.

In Bolshevia the attitude of the children towards the older generation is rather one of compassion. We say "he doesn't understand, he's only a child." In Bolshevia, in identically the same way, they say "he doesn't understand; he can't be expected to, he's too old." The hard fact that the older generation is antagonistic to Bolshevism has been faced, and the party communist is not ashamed that his old mother and old father are not communists. "It can't be helped; they can't be expected to understand everything." In political prosecutions age is regarded as a mitigating circumstance, just in the same way as extreme youth is taken into account in applying our penal code.

According to Soviet ideas, the individual should not expect to choose his work, his occupation, his profession, which is imposed on him from above. The communist always does that which the party orders him to do. Mr.

Arens, the chief of the Press department of the Soviet Foreign Office, a man who had always been a diplomat, was suddenly sent to the Ural mountains as financial controller of a factory—through no fault of his own, but only, so I was told (and I don't know in the least whether it is true), following rumours that he took part in the kidnapping of General Kutiepov. This is called "party discipline," and no one dares protest when he is sent off, heaven knows where, to an entirely different occupation, to a kind of work which is quite new to him, and which may be far beneath his qualifications. Besides this "party discipline" there exists another order, the "party over-load" (*partinaja nagruzka*), which requires that every communist, *komsomolets*, student, schoolboy, and even member of a trades union, shall perform certain work without pay—work which is sometimes very hard. It may consist of unloading wagons and carrying sacks; it may consist of being told off to catch *bezprizorni* (parentless children) in all sorts of places.

Those who did not know Russia before the Revolution may not know to what extent the Russian "intellectual" was an individualist—Pushkin, Lermontov, Schedrin, Turgeniev, Alexander Tolstoy, Leo Tolstoy, Tchekov, were all individualists, anarchists. They permitted no dictation where they themselves were concerned; indeed, they were constantly pre-occupied with the question whether they were really free. For example, during the Russo-Japanese War an officer of the Russian army, who was also a writer —a writer, be it noted, not in the first rank and having no claims to be a genius—wrote a novel in which he glorified a Japanese spy. This spy was sleeping in a house of ill-fame, and in his sleep called out *banzai*, which betrayed him to the girl he was with. She denounced him to her lover, a member of the Russian Secret Service. The Japanese jumped out of the window and broke his leg, but continued to act as a hero. The Japanese was, in fact, the hero of the novel, and was described with warmth and sympathy by the author—and this was a novel written by a Russian officer during the war with Japan. The Russian intelligentsia has paid dearly for this anarchy of thought, for its lack of patriotism, for its betrayal of its Tsar. But what a contrast we see to-day! Set against the undisciplined liberalism of the novel by Kuprin, the following example from contemporary Russia provides a striking testimony to the change that has come about!

Along the whole length of a block of flats hangs a long banner with the words: "A clean-up is being held in the House-Building Institute in

Moscow." What does this mean? It means that in the House-Building Institute there is being held an investigation to see whether any of the employees is a *lishenets*, an "outlaw," or is a son of a *kulak*; to see whether they really all are convinced communists. Of course, during this "clean-up" the slightest hesitation, the slightest ground for suspicion, result in dismissal—and the loss of bread cards, etc.; for the reduction of a certain number of employees must be justified somehow. But no one is ashamed that this "clean-up" is going on; on the contrary, it is greeted joyfully and triumphantly, and a huge red banner hangs all the length of the house. People, rejoice! A clean-up is going on!

In old Russia it was considered desirable to have a certain section of the youth of the country on the side of the Government. This purpose was served by the *corps de pages*, the *lycée*, and the legal schools. The means adapted to instil loyalty to the dynasty was an education in which the tradition of the school, the *esprit de corps* in the military academy or the regiment was held sacred. But the old methods pale into insignificance when compared with the present state of affairs. The privileged youth of the old *régime* produced the Princes Kropotkin, the founders of international anarchy; and the Empress Alexandra

Teodorovna was right when she declared that the grand dukes made the Russian revolution.

The present working-class youth in the schools also feels that it is privileged; but it is privileged to a different end, and its characteristic expression is opposition to all religion and a slavish admiration for the Soviet *régime*.

It is really only in the territory of the U.S.S.R. that one realizes to the full what a tragedy it is to be old. The age at which one is old is there a very low one—thirty years. The man of thirty well remembers pre-war times, the prosperity, the "voluntary" freedom (for so the Bolsheviks call freedom of movement and freedom to live as one wants to), the freedom to think, to write, the freedom of art—in general, he well remembers those "bad old times," those times of Tsarist tyranny and political pressure. He compares them with these times of Bolshevik "freedom"—and cannot understand the young generation. Everything is so changed. There is a drama of Tchekov's in which an old serving-man weeps while the old cherry-trees are being chopped down in the garden. This drama is lived by every thirty-year-old person in Bolshevia every year. It ages him. We observe here the phenomenon that the circumstances of life bring about an intensified process of ageing in the case of pre-war people. The Bolshevik system is a kind of mass Voronov system *à rebours*.

The young generation has no basis for comparison; it is convinced that things were much worse formerly; that it is privileged. Romanticism, idealism, eroticism, feelings for women, the marriage triangle; these are all points of view that it despises. Bolshevik ideology has developed over the heads of its teachers. I have spoken of *esprit de corps*. Like everything in old Russia, the sacredly nursed feeling of *esprit de corps* turned against the masters, against authority. In the new schools in new Russia there is no whispering the answer to a question in a fellow pupil's ear, there is no conspiring amongst the pupils to cheat authority. On the contrary, the place of such practices has been taken by "self-criticism." I have already mentioned group rivalry as a powerful psychological factor which harnesses the Soviet machine to its work in the revolutionary atmosphere. A second example of the same method must not be overlooked. It is the "wall gazette." Each class at school has its "wall gazette," in which the behaviour of the pupils is criticized, their faults pointed out, and in which they criticize themselves. This system of self-criticism and "wall-gazettes" is universal in Government offices and in factories; and even in the army every company, every battery or squadron has its "wall-gazette." I saw a "wall-gazette" in the editorial offices of the *Izvestia.* It was edited by the compositors. The day I saw it one of the members of the staff had written an article in which the words growth, grow, grew, etc., were constantly repeated. The article had been stuck on to the "wall-gazette," the repeated expressions underlined, and by the side of it had been drawn a caricature of the author of these errors of style with the heading "How Comrade X grew"—Comrade X (I did not note his name) was shown in the caricature with a long-drawn-out neck.

The present system intensifies Bolshevism and socialism—and thereby reduces them to an absurdity. Some talk of doing away altogether with money; attempts have been made to convert villages into living communes—and are still being made. But there is one direction in which the Bolsheviks have not been consistent. The abolition of private property, the institution of life in communes, into which with the expenditure of so much effort the Bolsheviks are trying to force their citizens, cannot, in my opinion, be put through successfully without the communization of women, without unregulated polygamy and polyandry. But this has not been effected, and the line of development of the relations between the sexes takes rather the opposite direction, is reactionary.

The reason is woman.

Not that I believe that woman instinctively defends monogamy. No. This is a matter not of woman defending her own husband, but her own child. The flooding of Bolshevia by parentless children is passing. There are hardly any of these parentless children left now, compared with two years ago. And as a matter of fact, a great number of them were the children of people thrust out of the normal course of their lives during the period of militant communism, or of people who had been shot. Woman in Bolshevia obtained equal rights with man, not only juridically, but also practically. A woman may be, and often is, an officer in the army. I have seen women cavalry officers. But, as I have said, my opinion is that this union will only last for a certain time. The Bolsheviks to-day regard as their greatest enemies, on the one hand, the idea of Russian chauvinism, and on the other *petit bourgeois* instincts. What they call *petit bourgeois* instincts cannot be exorcised from women. Here the revolution will find itself opposed to an obstacle which it cannot surmount. The women will not give up the right of possession of the young child.

The expressions "idealism," "idealist" are offensive in Soviet Russia. At a meeting of communist literary men I said, "I call idealists people who go hungry and without clothes, and suffer it enthusiastically because the five years' plan is progressing." And really, I cannot call the Bolsheviks anything else but idealists. The existence itself of this huge State, which voluntarily writhes in nightmarish tortures, is a proof that the man who declares that the life of classes, societies and nations is regulated solely by economic and material considerations, is an absolute fool. If it were true, how could there exist this phenomenon of a people of 160 millions voluntarily living in poverty?

In the same way, the thesis that the age of religion has passed finds no support in the Soviet State. The European reader may not know that *moshchi* is an embalmed body which the pious make pilgrimages to see. "The same religion—the same relics," said a lady to me in Moscow with a sarcastic smile, referring to the mausoleum of Lenin, which is in the centre of the Red Square, where there is always a long queue of people desirous of seeing the embalmed body of the leader, a queue which reaches as far as the church of Vassily Blazhenny, and there dwindles away. Since the death of the Prophet, day after day, day after day, this pilgrimage goes on. How many tens of millions of people have passed in front of that glass sarcophagus?

There is a quiet but persistent rumour that the Lenin lying there, which the passing throng is not allowed to examine too closely, is not Lenin, but only a wax effigy. Whether this is true or not, the fact remains that the uttering of this suggestion in Moscow is regarded as *treason* of the worst category. If it should, however, prove to be true, and the figure is really only an effigy of Lenin, an investigation into the matter would not resemble an inquiry into the authenticity of a museum specimen. By no means. It would be a matter of the greatest political import, a constitutional matter. How little this all fits in with the idea of an exclusively materialistic state and society!

CHAPTER IX

PALIMPSEST

SOMEONE started the idea, and lots of people have adopted it, that the Bolsheviks treat their museums in a cultured manner. This is utterly unfounded. It is true that the Bolsheviks did not tear the Rembrandts in the Ermitage to ribbons to give them to the people for wrapping round their feet. If anyone considers this a positive service to culture, I won't quarrel with him. But the furniture from the Tsar's palaces has been removed to the workmen's clubs and, of course, has been damaged by the public. And the Winter Palace in Leningrad with its beautiful *parquetterie* has been converted into a museum of the revolution, pounded daily by thousands of heavy boots, destroyed in a senseless and stupid fashion. And the most beautiful Gobelins, the finest pictures, may at any moment be thrust aside or obscured by placards stuck over with penny-halfpenny revolution photographs. The descriptions of the works of art in all the beautiful museums of Russia are universally associated with anti-religious and anti-bourgeois propaganda.

Let us add a reference to the sale of canvases

and *chefs d'œuvre* practised on a large scale by the Bolsheviks. These works of art are exported abroad and sold to find the money for industrializing the country.

I retain my objectivity to the end. I travelled to Moscow and Leningrad direct from Rome. I had clearly in my mind's eye the ruins of the temples, the baths, the pagan buildings demolished by the emancipated Christians. There, also, were lost many, many of the objects of ancient culture.

But there is a difference. Christianity demolished that which contradicted the idea of the soul. Bolshevism smashes and crushes what contradicts the most materialistic conception the world has ever seen.

But people like Bruno Jasinski, who hate Christianity, are Bolsheviks, and rave about the pagan world, the world of antique culture, are ridiculous. How absurd their misunderstanding! The antique world was a world of culture, a world of artistic beauty. Bolshevism, with the whole force of its thick-skinned ideology, turns against that very world. Bolshevism is the denial of and the fight against all that is artistic, all that is beautiful. Paganism, in order to erect one building, was willing to send to their death a thousand slaves. Bolshevism, to save a single factory, is ready to sacrifice not one cathedral in Rheims, but all the cathedrals in Europe and all the sculpture in the world.

There are no greater extremes than the world of antique culture and the destroyers of all culture, prosperity and freedom for mankind—the Bolsheviks.

I would like to reply to my fifth and last question, about the palimpsest. The reader will himself, however, have found the answer in what I wrote about fellow-travellers and about the nationality policy of the Soviets. We saw that literature and art generally are forced brutally into accord with the requirements of propaganda for the class-war and the needs of the moment of the Soviet State. Free art is trampled down, and, in particular, any signs of a connection with the ideas of former Russian literature are crushed. In respect of national minorities, the Bolsheviks pursue a policy which I call the "Demian's Soup" policy. This is the title which Krylov gave to his story of the hospitable host who stuffs his guest with so much fish soup—with more and still more spoonfuls of this Russian delicacy—that the unhappy guest flees, and from that time on never revisits Demian. The national minorities, beginning with the Ukraine, have in the way of languages received more than they can digest. Born Russians, on territory reorganized as minority territory, are forced to speak Ukrainian, White Russian, Tatar, and dialects which yesterday possessed no alphabet. In this manner, I repeat, the national minorities have, as far as languages are concerned, been given more than they can digest. But at this price has been stultified the development of their own nationalism, their own patriotism. The idea of Stalin—that the culture of these minorities should be national in form but Soviet in substance—has been realized.

This could not be done with the Russians. It was obviously out of the question to institute any policy of extension of the language rights of the Russian language. Besides which, in strength and quality the Great Russian nation cannot be compared with the other nationalities of the Soviet State. The Russian neo-patriotism hung over the heads of the Soviets like the sword of Damocles. To-day this Russian neo-patriotic movement scarcely exists. I have mentioned that 70 per cent of the inhabitants of Russia are inimically disposed towards the authorities, although they are absolutely impotent, passive. But this patriotism may be resurrected. A shock of some kind may occur which will wake it up. The only alternative to the Bolshevik ideology would seem to be a Russian imperial ideology—and I personally am prepared to support the view that it would be on a historical foundation, based on an admiration for Ivan III and Peter, and even Nicholas I, with a monarchist complexion.

On my way to Bolshevia I had a discussion with a Bolshevik who officially lived in Warsaw, and explained to him my theory of the palimpsest—that under a Bolshevik veneer I should find a layer of old Russia—unchangeably Russian. I did not know at the time that the announcement of such a quest—that I proposed to prove the existence of what is most of all repressed and persecuted in Russia—would sound like provocation. Before I went to Russia, too, I had the intention of writing a sketch about a contemporary Soviet author under the title: "A noble puppy." The author in question had written many things against the bourgeois, but I wanted to prove that in the stream that flowed from his pen there were threads that justified my title. I shall not refrain from writing such a sketch simply from motives of decency. The author I had in mind has been arrested, and my article, translated by the G.P.U., would have afforded additional material for the charges against him.

So much for the palimpsest.

CHAPTER X

TERRORISM

I AM often asked: Are the Soviets more open to attack by terrorism than the old Russian *régime?* And are they likely to sustain such a shock as would shatter their power?

I will confess that I prefer giving information about Bolshevia to constructing theories and hypotheses. It is so difficult to construct an hypothesis when one is standing on that volcanic ground where the earth trembles under one's feet, where everything changes from minute to minute.

I imagine, however, that if anyone cared to carry it out a centralized organization of terrorism of the members of the Government and of the central institutions and offices in Moscow would have very great effects. (I apologize to our Ministry of Foreign Affairs for permitting myself to consider such a suggestion in relation to the affairs of a neighbouring State; although, while I was in Moscow, I saw so many efforts directed towards world revolution and heard so many insults to my own country that even if I did urge the application of terrorism in Russia I should be justified on the principle of reciprocity—with plenty to spare. But, in fact, I only mention the possibility in an attempt to elucidate the question of what might conceivably happen to the Soviets.)

I imagine that a sufficiently intensified and concentrated terrorism would do more damage to Bolshevism than was suffered by the old Russian *régime* from the bombs that were thrown at Plehve, Sipiagin, etc. The difference is accounted for by the leaders' own sense of their importance to their enemies. The Bolsheviks have not in their own country any strong anti-Bolshevik organizations. The Tsarist Government was aware of the internal opposition to its policy, and consequently was conscious of the power it wielded. It even vastly over-estimated its importance. Tsar Nicholas II in Tobolsk was convinced that the Germans wanted to capture him and force him to sign the treaty of Brest. This was an example of his exaggerated sense of power. But it is a strange thing that the Bolshevik leaders not only do not possess this sense, but are all the time speaking and thinking in terms of the importance of their enemies. Indeed, the possibility present in their minds of Bolshevism being overthrown has something in it of a vision seen in a dream; no one knows how it arises, but it exhausts and suffocates like a nightmare.

Writing this, I again have in mind the "old" Bolsheviks. I have already drawn attention to the difference between the old Bolsheviks and Bolshevik youth. Bolshevik youth has outdistanced its leaders both in matters of doctrine and in its application to the uttermost consequences. Bolshevik youth is obtaining more and more posts, and constantly more important posts, in the work of the State—which means, in Bolshevia, work in general. But the highest offices, such as the *Sovnarkom* of the U.S.S.R., or the Council of Ministers, are still filled by older men And it is on those latter that terrorism would have an effect. It would be a too simple explanation to say that they would be afraid or anything like that. But in view of the feeling of the uncertainty of their position which these men always have (they constantly think of war, of strengthening their power, of *coups d'état* against internal opposition), they would, under the pressure of violence, break down psychologically, as did Louis Philippe and Alfonso XIII.

And then, that which to-day is the centre of power would become a centre of panic. The panic would radiate from the central point, from the nerve of authority, from the brain of authority. It could paralyse the whole organism.

In five or ten years' time youth will have

taken over all the offices in Bolshevia. So that both as regards the danger of war and the danger of terrorism, time works on the side of the Bolsheviks.

Once more I would like to repeat, in order to amplify my point, that a tremendous amount of thought and work is devoted by the Bolshevik leaders simply to making their position more and more secure. The *Kolchozes*, the five years' plan, the reorganization of industry—what is this all from the psychological point of view? It has the same motive as that system of moving from town to town of the furniture taken from private people. In the same way as no one in Soviet Russia could to-day identify his former chair or his cupboard, so the whole social and industrial structure of the country is being so changed that "its own mother wouldn't know it"—and a return to the old conditions is impossible on mere technical or material grounds.

In point of fact, as far as the danger of terrorism is concerned, it seems to me that the Bolsheviks need not fear it. It is simply inconceivable that a plot could be organized either abroad or in Bolshevia—at least without the aid of an *agent-provocateur*. The old Russian parties employed *agents-provocateurs*, but the Bolsheviks have perfected this system. In comparison with the

Bolsheviks, the old Tsarist Government dealt with political offenders with gloves on; indeed, there was a sort of moral obligation to help political offenders during the Tsarist *régime*. Every noble, every merchant, every other bourgeois helped them to escape, even though they aimed at destroying the bourgeoisie. To-day a genuine counter-revolutionary would be seized by the first *komsomolets* or *komsomolka* he met.

I do not believe that the Russian *émigrés* are seriously capable of fighting the Soviets. I have even heard it said that General Kutiepov was organizing a fight by terrorism, and that for that reason he was kidnapped. The Bolsheviks will seize or kill everyone who is really a dangerous opponent.

CHAPTER XI

THE FUTURE

WHILE repeating my dislike of theorizing about Russia, instead of giving information about that country, I must, however, put my impressions in order and suggest what may happen to that empire.

1. The most probable development, *in spite of everything*, I consider to be the fall of the Soviets, caused by some cataclysm, the nature of which it is very difficult to foresee. It is not to be imagined that a consistently drugged society can exist for long, and these everlasting changes, this revolutionizing of everyday life, is really a kind of drug—a drug which is destructive in its effects, and is not favourable to life.

2. The second possibility is the victory of the Soviets and the idea of Bolshevism over the whole globe. Two ways might lead to this: there is the infection that I will call business short-sightedness, which poisons the *defensive* power of our world against Bolshevik aggression, and there is the infection of ideas which enables the Bolsheviks to penetrate our world with an *offensive* of ideas.

3. The third possibility would be that of Capitalism existing side by side with Bolshevism. With such a revolutionism as exists in Russia to-day, such a side-by-side existence could last ten, fifteen, even twenty years. But it would finish by aggression on the part of the Bolsheviks. Both the N.E.P. (new economic policy) and the five years' plan are only breathing-spaces for them.

My personal view of the political psychology of the Middle Ages, of the Renaissance and of the present day—a view which I do not propose here either to justify or to develop—sees it under two aspects, the noble-military and the merchant-bourgeois. Historically this division has persisted from the Middle Ages. To the first aspect belongs, in my opinion, the political innovator. The distinction I make corresponds to the division between ambition for power and hunger for money. My thesis is that not economics but politics, or problems of power, have governed the world; and that politics, or the desire for power, created one or another kind of economic situation. The greatest representative of military psychology was Napoleon. The period of the greatest hegemony of the mercantile spirit is the present day, beginning with the Treaty of Versailles.

Leaving the field of aphorisms for a moment, I will cite a little rhyme which I found in the memoirs of one of the most interesting figures in Polish politics. This rhyme exactly characterizes the relationship between the military psychology and the business psychology, as I understand it. It is very deep, this rhyme—which as a matter of fact is based on Pushkin.

"All is mine"—said the sword.
"All is mine"—said the gold.
"I'll take all"—said the sword.
"I'll buy all"—said the gold.
"Off you go"—said the sword.
"Well, I'll go"—said the gold.

The Tories and Liberals are all on the same side. Sometimes those who are really only representatives of monetary interests consider themselves Conservatives. In Poland the right "national" party is at the same time an extreme pro-Bolshevik party in international politics. I regard only those as real Conservatives, however, who are able to distinguish between these mixed elements.

The merchant who goes to Bolshevia does not understand that he represents an uneven side, an unevenly weak side. He only wants to make money, and goes there only in his capacity of a merchant. But he has to deal with a man who is of iron as far as his ideology of communist aggression is concerned.

I wish to refer here to a matter which concerns me closely—the impression aroused by my articles. It is true that I have written the truth, for I hold that every deviation from the truth increases the danger with which we are threatened by Bolshevism. And, just because I was telling the truth, I described in all his horror the creature who is not only hungry and ill-clothed, but also has all his ideas fixed as in a vice. He is a man undergoing the worst form of forced imprisonment, for he is undergoing mental hard labour. And yet I hear that my studies are regarded by one very great man as encouraging to Bolshevism. And I have read an article written by a lady in which, while writing very favourably about me, she makes me out to be a Bolshevik propagandist.

I am unable to explain this phenomenon otherwise than by a Bolshevik infectious bacillus, a kind of brain illness that is to be met with in people eating white rolls and drinking coffee on the banks of the Seine, the Vistula and the Thames. Anatole France, that great pagan, praised Bolshevism! Whence comes this bacillus? I venture to say that it comes from satiety of prosperity. Here we talk of poverty, unemployment, the economic crisis, and the catastrophic situation. Go to Bolshevia. Then you will call everything that is happening to us: satiety of prosperity.

CHAPTER XII

CONVERSATION IN A TRAIN

A FEW words about Sokolov's book, *The Murder of the Imperial Russian Family*.

After Ekaterinburg had been freed from the Bolsheviks, the Russian authorities (on July 30th) instructed the public prosecutor for specially important cases, Mr. Nametkin, to investigate this case. Mr. Nametkin was a judge residing in Ekaterinburg, and did not wish to undertake the case without the instructions of the public prosecutor of the court in question, as was the usual procedure in Russian criminal cases. His successor was Mr. Siergieyev, a member of the court, and *his* successor was Mr. Sokolov, a *juge d'instruction* of the Omsk court. The results of his investigations, which were strictly those of a court of investigation, together with his own personal opinions of a historical character—even of a politico-historical character—are published in his book, under the title given above.

At the beginning of this book Mr. Sokolov underlines:—

"I do not pretend to know all the facts, or to have brought the whole truth to light. I only assert that I am the one who has got the nearest to the truth."

To these words, written in 1924, history has been able to add nothing, for one cannot take seriously for a moment the fantastic story of Mme. Czajkovska, who pretends that she is Anastazia, the daughter of Nicholas II, although she neither speaks Russian nor English, and does not remember the names of any towns in Russia except St. Petersburg, and has further been demasked by her sister as one Anna Szanekovska, of Silesia. The results of Mr. Sokolov's investigations can, however, thanks to a curious combination of circumstances, be added to in a few particulars. Mr. Sokolov has established the identity of the guard which guarded the Imperial Family in Ekaterinburg, and the names are to be found in his book. They only refer, however, to the detachments formed at the Zlotokasovov and Syssert works. According to Mr. Sokolov's investigations, these detachments were, several days before the murder, transferred to outside duties in the garden near the fence, while the indoor service, the direct guarding of the Tsar and his family, was taken over by Chekists (members of the Cherezvychaika). When exactly this took place Mr. Sokolov did not establish, but on p. 172 of his book he relates that in the first days of July the commandant of the house of Ipatiev, one Avdieyev, was replaced by Jacob Jurovski, whose assistant was one Nikulin. Further, Mr. Sokolov writes, several days later these two were joined by ten men who lived on the ground floor in rooms Nos. 2, 4 and 6.

The names of these men Mr. Solokov could not establish. Later on in his book he establishes that they were Chekists, and that, under the leadership of Jurovski, they carried out the actual crime. Mr. Sokolov regards Jacob Jurovski (a Jew) as their leader. This book contains, in my opinion, too few proofs to contradict my discovery, viz., that the actual leader of this band of Chekists was not Jurovski, but a certain Grishka Suchorukov. The name Grishka would appear to have been fatal indeed for the last Tsar of all the Russias.[1]

My fellow-traveller mentioned the name Jurovski to me, but not as the chief. I must point out that Sokolov underlines the fact that among the twelve Chekists there were several Letts, and also considers that there was a Hungarian, and cites rhymes written on the walls in German. I inquired specially about the Hungarian. My informant told me that there was no Hungarian, and generally no ex-prisoner of war

[1] This was, of course, the Christian name of Rasputin.

among them. It was a "northern punitive detachment of the Cheka." I imagine that the emphasis which Sokolov places on the presence of foreigners amongst the band of murderers of the Tsar arose from Mr. Sokolov's patriotism—before which I bow my head. I am sorry to dispel this illusion, and would add that I use the word "illusion" without any shadow of offence, but with the greatest respect and sincere sympathy. I understand quite well the excellent monarchical patriotism of unhappy old Russia.

Since we are discussing the sentiments of Mr. Sokolov I must, by way of digression, illustrate just one other hypothesis of his, which he develops in his book, but which does not come within the strict sphere of his investigations, i.e. Ekaterinburg. Throughout the whole of his book there stands out the conviction that one Yakovlev, who convoyed the Tsar, the Tsarina and the Grand Duchess Marie, was a German agent who worked to save the Tsar, but that when it was found that the Tsar refused the German's offer, Yakovlev left him to his fate in Ekaterinburg. Without going any closer into this hypothesis, I will merely state that I asked my informant if he knew the Yakovlev who convoyed the Tsar from Tobolsk to Ekaterinburg. He replied that he knew him, and even gave me his present address, namely, Shantash in the Urals, as far as I remember on the banks of a lake of that name, where he is engaged in market gardening.

Mr. Sokolov in his book says that he cannot describe the murder authentically, but gets his idea of it from an examination of the interior of the room in which the murder took place, and from an examination of witnesses, none of whom, however, were actual eye-witnesses of the crime, but simply repeated to the investigating judge what they had heard at second or third hand. Mr. Sokolov never saw a single member of the band of Chekists who committed the crime; he further knew none of their names, apart from Jurovski and Nikulin. Finally, he did not know who gave Jurovski—whom he wrongly considers the chief of the band—the order to commit the murder, or on whose authority.

My information clears up this point. It appears that Nicholas II and his family were murdered as the result of a misunderstanding. Having said so much, I will proceed to describe in detail the circumstances in which this information was given to me.

On the 5th of May, 1931, I got into the mail train at Kazan, due to leave Kazan at 8.40 local time. This train came in forty minutes late. In one of the upholstered carriages there travelled with me actors of the Little Theatre and of the Moscow Art Theatre, who were returning from a tour of the *Kolchozes*. These were, of course, not the best actors from their theatres, but special "brigades" as they call them, sent out to do propaganda in the depths of the country. One of these actors was formerly a homeless orphan (*bezprizorny*), and one of them was even a witness of the most interesting parts of my conversation. I learned the name of this actor—an elderly man, who said he had known Mr. Lednicki. His name was Nicholas Fogt. My informant was not an actor, but was journeying from Sverdlovsk to Moscow to attend a congress. As often happens when travelling in Russia, he talked a lot. At first I did not attach any special importance to what he was saying, and although he showed me his card of identity as a member of his *gorsoviet* —town council—in Sverdlovsk, I did not even pay any attention to his name. But later, when I learned that he was chairman of the commission for "cleaning-up" former partisans, that he lived in the house for former Chekists in Sverdlovsk, and that during the whole Russian civil war he had been a member of the "Northern punitionary detachment of the Cheka," I began to observe him closer. He then showed me his identity card as chairman of the "cleaning-up" commission;

his name was Makiadan. I must here remark that Sverdlovsk is identical with Ekaterinburg, being the new name of that city.

The story which Makiadan told during that day which I spent in the same compartment with him was more or less as follows:—

He was born in Moldavia. He still hankered after Moldavia, and would have liked to go there, but could not get a foreign passport. In Moldavia he had a father aged ninety-four and a mother aged eighty-two, whom he would like to see. He also had relatives in Poland—a lawyer named Gaberski, living in Lublin and married to a Miss Jankovska from Kisheniev, who was Makiadan's relative.

He also told me about his wife, the daughter of a veterinary surgeon from Petrograd, who was herself a qualified veterinary surgeon; how he met her in 1920 or 1921 while travelling by train at the head of a detachment of the Cheka, and how he afterwards married her; how he had two children, the elder of whom he wanted to send to school. As, however, the members of the Cheka house had no school of their own, he tried to send him to a railwayman's school, but the latter would not take a boy who was not a railwayman's child.

During the war he had been wounded three

times, and he showed me a scar on his left hand from a bullet wound which had passed through it. He had not served in the Russian army during the Great War. His age was thirty-two. He owned a gold watch presented to him by Trotsky.

At one moment in the conversation I said I regretted that I had not been able to visit Sverdlovsk, and had not seen Ipatiev's house. And then like a flash of lightning it passed through my mind.

"So you were there . . . then. . . ."

"Of course we were."

And then he began to tell me all about it.

In the evening a telegram had come from Bieloborodov from Bashenov, a place about thirty miles from Ekaterinburg. The telegram stated that the enemy were pressing, and contained at the end the phrase "take the necessary measures."

"Sukhorukov then collected all twelve of us to consider what was to be done. You understand that killing the Tsar was not killing me, or you. I took no part in the discussion; I had a sore throat and could not talk. Well, we decided that it was necessary to kill him. Bieloborodov came the next day, and when he saw they were all dead, he cursed us properly. 'You all deserve shooting,' he said."

"And Jurovski was there?" I asked.

"Yes, he was."

"At midnight Sukhorukov went to them and told them that their rooms were to be disinfected. He talked of disinfection, but they felt that something was amiss. I was on the stairs as they passed down. Nicholas, his wife, and the four young ladies. They were so pretty. . . ."

I remember how I shuddered when Makiadan said "they were so pretty." I thought of the feelings of a man watching four girls—princesses—being led to butchery.

"As far as the attendants were concerned, they condemned themselves to death. We said: 'Attendants outside,' but they replied, 'We won't go.' The doctor also was there, Dr. Botkin. 'Well, if you won't go, the devil take you.' You understand, shooting twelve people was not the same as shooting seven. We wanted to take the others outside the house and let them go.

"It is not true that they were tormented. May boiling oil be poured on my hand if I'm not speaking the truth." (This is a common Russian oath.)

"When did you tell the attendants that they could go?"

"That was four o'clock. At midnight we brought them downstairs, and went to sleep. At four o'clock we went in, and Sukhorukov said: 'Now you can go,' and they said: 'We won't go.' "

"People say that a sentence was read, and that the Tsar was told, 'We must shoot you,' and that he said, 'What!' . . .

"Nonsense. Nothing of the sort. We fired, and that was all."

"And did the Tsar hold the Tsarevitch by the hand?"

"On the contrary, Nicholas was the first to fall. They were all in their nightdresses; the girls had flannel dressing-gowns on. One of the girls was hit in the arm, and was fired at twice. The Tsarevitch was fired at four times. He seemed to stiffen, and then a bullet hit him above the ear. . . . In their dressing-gowns we afterwards found a lot of diamonds."

"And what happened to their clothes? Part of their clothes were found together with the burnt bodies."

"We took their clothes out to burn everything together."

"And they say that one of the servant girls and one of the princesses were killed with bayonets?"

"Nothing of the sort. No one touched a bayonet." In Makaidan's voice there was the same sincere pathos when he made this assertion as when he insisted that no one tormented them. As if to kill a person with a bayonet was a serious crime compared with merely shooting them.

He afterwards described the details of the burning of the bodies. As far as I could understand—and I was rather upset at what I had heard—his report coincided with Sokolov's.

I don't remember quite how the conversation turned on the Grand Duke Michael Alexandrovitch.

"He was killed on the eleventh day after Nicholas. He was killed in the courtyard of the theological seminary."

As far as I know, this is the first news as to the place where the Grand Duke Michael Alexandrovitch was murdered. Hitherto all that was known was that he was last seen at Perm.

CHAPTER XIII

THE THREE CAUSES OF THE CATASTROPHE

THIS "Casual Conversation in a Train" finds a place quite by chance in my observations on Bolshevia. It rather clashes with the "publicist" nature of those observations, being rather a page torn from a reporter's note-book. But it will serve as a connecting link with a few remarks I would like to make about "submerged Russia." How did it all happen? The February revolution was brought about by an act of terrorism in which one of the Grand Dukes took part (the murder of Rasputin), and it united all classes of Russian society against one man, or rather, against that man and his wife. In order to push down the obstacle that stood in the way of the normal development of Russia everybody exerted such an effort that together with the obstacle they fell over the precipice.

A terrible curse seems to hang over everything one reads about Nicholas II and over everything one learns from those who knew him. He was an autocrat ruling one-sixth of the globe. His every word was an act that could have enormous significance for the lives of thousands of people.

His every error, slip, or carelessness revenged itself terribly on his people. It is for this reason that his former ministers—not the revolutionaries—have said such bitter things about him. But let us be more considerate than the representatives of the highest Russian bureaucracy.

Nicholas II was a gentleman in the full sense of that word. His "party," if such a word may be used, was an extremely reactionary one, although it included many men of unusual intelligence, and it regarded the war with Germany as a stupid adventure. He himself, being a reactionary to the bone, understood well the significance of a war between the last conservative monarchies of Europe. As the war went on he must have understood it more and more clearly. And yet in what a decided manner, with what horror he turned down every peace proposal, considering that he could not betray his allies. There was something in him of Paul I, something of his conception of Maltese honour in the blind way in which Nicholas II carried on the war, ruining Russia, the throne and himself. Let us bow our heads before his conception of the word of a Tsar—but not before his political insight. In defence of his political standpoint, it may be added that the whole Russian intelligentsia regarded the idiotic—as Count Witte quite correctly, from the Russian point of view, described it—war with Germany as the salvation of Russia.

In all that I have written about Bolshevia I have tried to sketch main characteristics, thickening in the dominating lines of the psychology that is governing the Soviets. I have filled in the details only as illustrations of what I might call the governing ideas. In this short note about the character of the last Tsar I try to keep to the same method, going no farther than to enumerate the fundamental characteristics of his psychology.

Nicholas II, then, was a man who was fond of family life, and who, had he not been Tsar, would never have occupied himself with public life, and would have wished nothing better from those around him than that he and his family should be left entirely alone. Fate, events, people, the Russian nation, did just the opposite; they directed a bright light on his private life, on everything that every man has the right to keep to himself; they advertised the most intimate things, pointed at them, exhibited them before the entire world.

The second characteristic of Nicholas II was his mysticism, which is an hereditary characteristic in the Romanov family. But Nicholas was the greatest mystic of them all—greater than Alexander I.

Isvolski relates how, during the first Russian revolution, the rebellious forts of Kronstadt were firing on the fleet, and how he, as Minister of Foreign Affairs, was making his report on consular affairs in Persia. The Tsar listened attentively, though the guns of Kronstadt were threatening not only the crown of Nicholas II, but also his life and the lives of his family, as in case of the success of the revolt, the road to the capital was cut off. Not until the report was finished, and the Tsar looked through the large window at the sea and the smoke of the firing, did Isvolski ask the Tsar why he was so calm. He received the reply, delivered in the most serious manner, that the Tsar was convinced that his fate, then as always, lay in the hands of God.

Nicholas II always had a deep presentiment that a tragic fate awaited him. Consequently, when the revolution broke out and he was dethroned, his family, almost with a feeling of relief, felt that "it has happened now."

Arising out of this mysticism there were two characteristics, one good and one bad. The good one was the deep feeling of Imperial responsibility. That insensibility, that unmoved tranquillity, that dignity, with which Nicholas II received the worst news; that quiet voice in which, when sitting down to lunch, he said: "I wonder how much longer Port Arthur will be able to hold out," simultaneously slipping under his napkin the telegram reporting that the Japanese had taken Port Arthur; that calm with which he met all the insults and chicanery after his dethronement—all came from the conviction that he was not an ordinary individual, but a man whom God had singled out for an extraordinary mission. He held to this belief with a childlike *naïveté*, or else with a mystical conviction worthy of admiration.

Apart from the sense of responsibility, the Tsar's mysticism created in him a belief in the Russian folk. He can be described as a kind of democrat—a peasant-maniac. No one can be quite free from the influence of his epoch, his age. The mysticism of Nicholas and his wife was mediæval. The Tsar kissed the hand of a kind of hermit, which had not been washed for fifty years. But this mediævalism was slightly tinged with Tolstoyism. Nicholas II, the reactionary, the mediæval mystic, had in many things a point of view similar to Tolstoy's. He hated the one-year conscripts, for they were the intelligentsia. He loved the private—the peasant soldier. He loved and believed in the Russian folk. He saw in them the haven of his God-sent mission.

Nicholas II's relations with Rasputin were

based on something deeper than an interest in spiritualistic séances. In that head, full of mediæval mysticism, of that suspicion of everyone surrounding him, so natural to an autocrat, and also of that literary belief in the Russian folk which was an unhealthy sign, a superstition almost, of the pre-war generation—in that head there grew a cult for Rasputin, the superman, the direct image of the religious and every other kind of opinion on the whole Russian folk.

Let us now turn directly to the catastrophic rôle which Nicholas II played in the life of the Russian State. Naturally, as the result of the characteristics which I have already outlined, Nicholas II was very far from sharing the convictions and the ideas professed during his reign by society in general in Russia. His ideas were at a very wide angle indeed from those of the Russian intelligentsia. There was an abyss between them which could not be crossed. With almost any other member of that dynasty on the throne, Russia would have had a better chance of escaping the catastrophe which overtook her. Nicholas II had absolutely no sense of reality; his was a fantastic mind, ready at every moment to believe every political fairy-tale. Such people occur not only on thrones, but also in everyday life, and even very often in political life, but of course they do not do so much damage. In Nicholas II's nature, with his natural, childish complaisance towards everything, there was also an exceptional horror of causing unpleasantness to anybody. He was ready to give way to everybody, to fall into line with everybody. These are the characteristics of a weak nature, and weak natures have also that tendency to go to the other extreme—a blind, senseless and immovable obstinacy. This is exactly the case with Nicholas II. His weakness, lack of strength of will, powerlessness to command, were combined with paroxysms of the most unbending obstinacy. These characteristics of his brought it about that during the Sturmer and Protopopov periods Russia found herself in a cul-de-sac.

On his dethronement Nicholas II became the redeemer of his faults and of the monarchy. Those characteristics which, while he was in power, brought about a catastrophe, then, on the contrary, worked for good. With dignity and calmness Nicholas II awaited death. Like the bouquets presented to an artist, the shedding of blood in connection with an ideal encourages and excites. The death of these girls, killed by the bullets that pierced their nightdresses and flannel dressing-gowns, still warm from sleep, did a greater service to the monarchical idea than did

Alphonso XIII with all his interviews and explanations in the newspapers. As a journalist emotionally bound to the monarchical idea, I would here like to underline this heavily.

CHAPTER XIV

THE RUSSIAN INTELLIGENTSIA

I HAVE said—cautiously enough—that with another Tsar Russia would have had a better chance of avoiding the revolution. If it had been Nicholas Nicholayevitch, he would have ruled as an autocrat, but as a talented and popular autocrat. If it had been Michael Alexandrovitch, the Tsar's brother, the Russians would have had a constitutional Tsar, similar in his behaviour to King George V. If it had been Constantine Constantinovitch, Europe would have seen a monarch who was a patron of the arts, somewhat of the type of the historically famous Grand Duke of Weimar.

But could all these "ifs" have changed the course of history? The Russian intelligentsia lacked to a degree the sense of duty towards the State—or, rather, were essentially anti-patriotic. Various nations give the name "intelligentsia" to different sections of society. In Russia, it had the widest possible signification. It included everybody outside the "folk," the masses—up to the highest sections of the bureaucracy. In other words, the intelligentsia did not include the peasant, the labourer, the minister of State, the heads of the police departments, the chiefs of staff. But the merchant who read Dostoyevski, the officer who attended the theatre—they all belonged to the intelligentsia. In justification of the attitude of this intelligentsia, it might perhaps be said that they over-estimated the importance and strength of the autocracy. Therefore everybody who took a hand in the fight against the autocracy was regarded by the intelligentsia as a "fellow-traveller" as the present-day Russian phrase goes.

Every anti-state organization found sympathy amongst the Russian intelligentsia. The Polish "sharp-shooters" movement was moneyless. Poland had at that time many rich citizens, many generous ones, but none of them were willing to give anything, for the "sharp-shooter" movement in those days was near to socialism. Pilsudski in his work for independence had to count literally upon every vote. From the history of the Russian socialist parties we know that those parties had at their disposal thousands of votes. Moreover, not only did thousands of gold roubles pour in from the secret police for the use of the social revolutionaries in organizing their acts of terrorism; they flowed in also from the pockets of the rich manufacturers, landed proprietors, well-to-do lawyers, doctors—from all those who have so much to thank the revolution for! Shcheglovitov, the Tsar's Minister of Justice, imprisoned in the Peter and Paul fortress by the Bolsheviks, while taking exercise in the prison courtyard, met Mr. Tereshchenko, a minister in the Prince Lvov Government, and a man well known formerly for his subsidies to the revolutionary movement. "They say," said Shcheglovitov to him, "that you paid five million roubles to get here. What a pity! Had I known earlier I would have put you here for nothing."

This anecdote has a symbolic character. I remember an article in the *Ryetch*, the organ of the Cadet party, on the centenary of the battle near Mozhaisk, at which Napoleon was defeated. The Cadets must be regarded as representing the average Russian intelligence. In that article the *Ryetch* had nothing other to say than that the French soldier in Russia felt like the Russian soldier in Manchuria—he was far from his country and let himself be beaten. This was all that the Russian intelligentsia had to say on the centenary of its country's glory. This was all that it had to say about the Asiatic problem which was of such great importance for Russia.

The Russian intelligentsia imagined that it was only anti-Government in the way it thought; but in fact it was anti-patriotic. The culminating manifestation of the atrophy of the sense of feeling for the country is, in my opinion, provided by the moment when, after the first Duma had been dissolved, Stolypin approached the parties in the Duma, and particularly the Cadets, with a proposal to form a Cabinet on a semi-parliamentary basis. The Tsar had been won over to this idea by Tropov. This fact alone relieves the last of the Tsars from a great deal of responsibility, and throws it on the Cadets, who *refused to agree to this proposal.* I can only once more repeat, the only motive that can be adduced in explanation of their attitude is that they overestimated the strength of the autocracy, that they regarded the autocracy as their one enemy, that they were convinced that on the fall of the autocracy the reins of government would pass into the hands of the intelligentsia, that they never dreamed of the bestial strength that raged in the crazy heads of the Russian subverts. For us Poles it is obviously better that the union of Stolypin with the Parliament did not come to fruition, but, in spite of all the pity which is deserved by a member of the intelligentsia—whether he be a beggar-outlaw in Russia or a chauffeur driving Americans to night-clubs in Paris—one cannot refrain from saying to him: "Tu l'as voulu, Georges Dandin."

Let us imagine that Nicholas II, when he became Tsar, instead of spending his time with his wife in nailing up pictures in their rooms, had gone to the Polytechnic in St. Petersburg and had addressed the lads there as follows: "Too long have we quarrelled. In Russia there is so much to be done. We have been outstripped by all the nations. We have a huge country, which waits for work, work and again work. We have Asia, which we should transform into another America." Naturally, had he had the nerve and the strength of Peter I he could have, even in 1894, done anything he liked with Russia. But it cannot be demanded of anybody that he should be able to do this. The best intentions and the most sensible action of an intelligent ruler were brought to naught by the anti-patriotic instincts of the Russian intelligentsia.

CHAPTER XV

"UNE STUPIDE AVENTURE"

THIS is what that great statesman, Serge Witte, called the Russo-German War. For us Poles it was blessed, as it gave us independence. But from the Russian point of view it was a madness—an "idiotic adventure," which was to push Europe into the power of the United States.

The expansion of a country should go in the direction which can give that country the most favourable results, and in a direction where there are the least obstacles to overcome. The turning of Russia against Germany, even in the case of victory, could not give Russia anything; and on the other hand, Russia met with the greatest possible resistance.

The explanation that Russia was interested in the Balkans, and that Russia fought the Germans as an ally of Austria, does not free Sazanov from the reproach of mistaken policy. First of all, Germany should have been divided from Austria by means of various concessions, if it were wished to carry through certain plans in the Balkans.

And what, after all, did her Balkan policy give Russia? Can the advantages which Russia might have obtained in the Balkans be compared with the advantages to be got from Asia, if a sensible policy had been pursued there? In my opinion, the policy of Alexander II is only a delayed execution of the plan of our King Ladislas IV. If Ladislas IV had been able to realize his plans, he would have created out of Poland a great empire. But in the time of Sazonov the value of the Balkans was quite a different one.

A proof of the logic of the thesis that the only rational direction for Russia to expand in is Asia, is provided by the contemporary policy of the Bolsheviks and its success.

INDEX